PAINTING BY NUMBERS

How to sharpen your BS detector and smoke out the "experts"

using examples drawn from polling data,
medicine, climate modeling, and more

JASON MAKANSI

Layla Dog Press

Layla Dog Press
Tucson, AZ 85719

Copyright © 2016 Jason Makansi

The author welcomes inquiries for professional and educational speaking engagements. Contact him directly at JMakansi@gmail.com.

For information, contact:
Layla Dog Press
1633 E Silver St, Tucson, AZ 85719
(an imprint of Blank Slate Communications LLC)
www.blankslatecommunications.com
www.paintingbynumbers.net
www.jasonmakansi.com
Manufactured in the United States of America
Cover Design by Elena Makansi
Interior Illustrations: Elena Makansi
Set in Adobe Caslon Pro and Raleway Regular

Library of Congress Control Number: 2016919996
ISBN: 978-0-9984259-0-0

For Munzer and Nellie Makansi, my father and mother

and

For Amira Kristine Makansi, Elena Katherine Makansi,
and Kristina Blank Makansi, the three lovely ladies
I live among, all three avid, successful writers

PAINTING BY NUMBERS

CONTENTS

Section II:
PUTTING YOUR BS DETECTOR TO WORK

PREFACE

I think it was third grade. Our teacher started a reading competition pledging to tape a square section (a "stage") of a rocket ship to the blackboard above our name for each book we read, but only after we wrote a brief summary proving we had read it.

I began reading books as fast as I could. To maintain my lead, I started "fudging" and read only the book's back flap to get enough for the summary. I wanted my rocket to reach the ceiling before my classmates.

I got one stage past the top of the blackboard before I got nailed. My teacher politely asked me if I had really read all those books in such a short time. She didn't have to ask twice before I confessed.

From this teachable moment, I learned valuable lessons about competition and lying. Though not cognizant of it at the time, I also learned about the power of representing numbers with pictures. Throughout my career, I've learned about the role of human bias in constructing a "mathematical model." But the first time I was conscious of it, the bias was mine.

As a high school senior with six college acceptances, my dad, a PhD chemical engineer, made me compare the schools based on a variety of parameters, such as location, reputation, cost, and several others. I had to rank each parameter from 1-10 for each school. If that wasn't enough, he made me create a weighting factor for each parameter's importance. As I proceeded through the exercise, I realized I had already made a selection in my mind and was subconsciously biasing the rankings to favor that school. This was a seminal moment. I became aware of how I was manipulating the numbers during an exercise designed for an "objective" answer. Much later in my career, I realized that companies, consultants, and government organizations pay millions of dollars to perform analyses not much more complicated than my college comparison, and usually full of similar built-in bias.

During college, many of the engineering courses I was required to take were of little practical use in my subsequent professional career. One course was a clear exception. It was a lab in which we had to perform a rigorous "error analysis" as part of every experiment. These were tedious, math-laden exercises, and aggravating. The laboratory equipment was antiquated and inaccurate, which introduced plenty of significant errors (in addition to the inherent error around every experiment).

Error analysis requires you to perform all the calculations twice. The first time is to determine the results, what you learned. That's hard enough. The second time, the error analysis, is to answer this question: How well do you know what you think you just discovered?

Error analysis taught me how to think critically about a numerical result. It taught me how to be a skeptic about the numerical results flying around me throughout life. It taught me how to be a skeptic, period.

Healthy skepticism proved eminently useful in my chosen career.

I wasn't the greatest engineering student. I was one of a few engineers, though, who loved to write. I might have been the only one in my class. It so surprised my engineering advisor, he asked me to help him edit an article for *Scientific American*. Sadly, he didn't finish his draft before I graduated. But he did let me fudge my electives so that liberal arts classes, which forced me to write papers every week, counted as "technical" electives.

In my first engineering positions, I quickly became known as the "guy who liked to write." Other engineers came to me with their reports and their presentations.

I began to learn how to interpret and convert into words what scientists and engineers were saying with numbers and math and graphs. In time, I entered the technical journalism/trade publication business. This required an ability to understand the science or technology, an ability to write about it, and a healthy skepticism to probe deeply and smoke out sales pitches, faulty information, and corporate, academic and professional jargon.

Today, numerical results hover around us daily, hourly even. We find them in articles in our social network feeds, newspapers and magazines, essays, television newscasts, professional publications, political discourse, and high level confabs with professional peers. Even casual discussions about sports inevitably revert to talk of "stats."

What's more, decisions based on numerical analysis and "algorithms" are being made for us in our digital worlds.

Rarely, however, does a thorough "error analysis" accompany these numbers, except perhaps in an academic setting. Information sources spend no time on "how well do we know this?" as they do on accentuating the positive, sensationalizing the results, or otherwise exaggerating to further professional goals and agendas—and grind political and cultural axes.

Throughout my career, I have been grateful for the

books and articles which simplify things rather than complicate them. I value authors who write to convey information to their audience, not to show how clever they are, prove to their boss how much they deserve a promotion, or demonstrate to their students how much more brilliant they are. I'll be honest, it took me a long time to learn this.

One of these books is Darrell Huff's *How to Lie with Statistics*. Originally published in 1954 and still selling today, with over half a million in sales ("An Honest to Goodness Bestseller," it says on the front cover), this little volume should be required reading for every American citizen—and citizens of any other country who can read English or get hold of a translated edition.

On page 2 of Mr. Huff's pocket-worthy tome are these words to live by:

"The secret language of statistics, so appealing in a fact-minded culture, is employed to sensationalize, inflate, confuse, and oversimplify. Statistical methods and statistical terms are necessary in reporting the mass data of social and economic trends, business conditions, 'opinion' polls, census figures. But without writers who use the words with honesty and understanding and readers who know what they mean, the result can only be semantic nonsense."

The distortions Huff cautions about have only gotten worse.

To make sense of modern life today, informed citizens have to go beyond statistics. Algorithms, computer programs, simulators, and other math, computer, and numerical "models" were once the purview of engineering, space program technocrats, remote pockets of academia, and the military, espionage, and defense industries. In other words, they once were the realm of the pocket protector crowd, of which I consider myself a proud member.

Today, numerical models have invaded our lives and the public square like weeds sprouting between the bricks along about mid-July.

On-line shopping, social media, automobiles and transportation, medicine and health, professional sports, environmental management, policy making, and virtually every other facet of our lives employ numerical models as a matter of course. Whole industries and services are being automated by algorithms, bots, and other digital tools and tricks of the trade.

But that's not the problem. The problem is that the public often accepts the output of these models as matters of fact. Experts deploy these models to advocate for a particular position, rather than research, investigate, and inform. Experts use models too often to divine the future, rather than explain the past, which is what models are good at.

Even baseball statistics have become unrecognizable from when I was dreaming about being a baseball star while fudging those book reports. Recently, I had the privilege of taking five representatives from overseas to an Oakland As—Houston Astros game, folks who had never been to a baseball game! A few days before the event, I started thinking about how to explain the game to them. It's one of the most complicated sports to make sense of.

I knew about Money Ball, Sabermetrics, and the new statistical framework around the game being used by owners, managers, and coaches, but only in general terms. I had always been pretty comfortable around runs batted in (RBI), slugging percentage, earned run average (ERA), on base percentage (OBP), and even on-base percentage + slugging (OPS).

I balked at the relatively recent, "wins above replacement," or WAR. This is described as a theoretical means of comparing any player to the "average" player at his position. You determine how many more games a team would have won if a player was replaced by the "average" player at his position. A player with a WAR (or WARP) value of 3 caused his team to win three additional games as a result of his play above the "replacement" level player.

It turns out there is no standard way to calculate WAR. It is described in Wikipedia as a "non-standardized Sabermetric baseball statistic." This beautifully reflects the problem with much quantitative and numerical analysis being used and abused today. There are few standards governing how numerical analysis is applied.

It's not just sports. Modern life is constructed with complex statistics and mathematical models as its foundation. Numerical analysis is fundamentally reshaping our society and our culture. Most everything you see in social media is a result of algorithms analyzing data.

All of your "digital actions" are being recorded. Your personal digital preferences are being used to "push" stuff at you, stuff your past actions suggest you will be interested in. In other cases, your data is aggregated and sanitized (to avoid privacy law violations) to reveal trends useful and valuable to others. From your iPhone to the iPad or laptop your doctor uses during your examination, data is being crunched everywhere!

What does all this "quant" stuff really tell us? How does it all serve us? How accurate is it? Does it inform debate or squash it? Do the numbers guys just win the argument?

Today, every citizen must be educated about how this data is analyzed behind the scenes and the limitations of those analyses.

Fortunately, you don't need to know much about math or quantitative analysis to think critically about numerical results. That's my goal with *Painting by Numbers*. Apply the twelve commandments outlined here, and you'll begin to think differently about the numbers bombarding you every day.

These twelve commandments are the tools of a healthy numerical skeptic.

You may not send away the "quant" quaking in his/ her boots. You will command more respect the next time you have to respond to a Powerpoint presentation. You'll feel better about everything bombarding you that is based on numerical analysis. Every numerical result, whether suggested by your doctor or repeated by your friends, should be filtered through these commandments.

Many fine books have been published recently dealing with the subject of math and computer models. I've provided a list of my favorites in Appendix 1. While I've found them enormously helpful and many of them eminently readable, they all have one or more of three primary limitations.

First, for the non-geek, those who are not comfortable with math, these books are too complex, even the ones which claim they are written for a "lay audience."

Second, several of them take aim at how models are used and abused in specific professions, most notably in financial engineering and Wall Street, environmental policy making, medicine, and digital life. The target readers for these books are professionals in these fields, although they may be enjoyed by non-professionals as well.

Third, while some books profess to be for a general readership (and a few do an excellent job), they still read more like textbooks or science books than a practical guidebook.

Sabermetrics may have changed the nature of managing baseball numerically, as opposed to managing players and a team. But the game will always boil down to fundamentals of running, hitting, catching, and throwing, skills most everyone can "get" with minimal effort.

In today's world, we need everyone to "get" the fundamentals of numerical analysis with minimal effort. After all, when the leader of the free world boils down to 0.045 percent of the votes cast in three key US states (based on the latest count before publication), and everyone across the political spectrum is astonished at the result, including the winner and virtually all the experts modeling the outcome, it's high time to pay at least as much attention to the tiny margin that spells victory or defeat as we do to the cadre of experts essentially amplifying the same results.

Before moving on, I want to be clear what this book is and is not.

It is intended to be a framework for better critical thinking about how numerical analysis is conducted, how results are turned into conclusions, and how all of it is delivered to an audience and ultimately converted into knowledge. It is not intended to be a means of science denial.

Painting by Numbers does not pretend to be an academic treatise or scholarly work. Think of it as your basic tool kit, adequate for performing home repairs, or at least staunching an emergency until professionals arrive. You should consider *Painting by Numbers* a prelude to the more thorough books listed in the Appendix 1.

The absence of positive examples of modeling and numerical analysis is deliberate. This is a book about the limitations in modeling and numerical analysis, limitations imposed by error and uncertainty in all its forms and the way numbers typically are reported to us. The intention is to heighten your situational awareness, and help you to understand how to question numbers as you come across them, not to teach you how to be a successful modeler or statistician.

Finally, this book in no way intends to disparage the use of statistics, numerical analysis and algorithmic modeling. When used correctly, they serve society well. This book is more a plea for recipients of numerical information to dig deeper for context and interpretation; for purveyors of numerical information to be more transparent about error, uncertainty, bias, and assumptions; and for everyone to be more sober about the actual insights which can be gained from the results and conclusions.

I sincerely hope *Painting by Numbers* will give you a better sense of how well you know what you think you know, and to appreciate the painstaking process behind achieving some measure of consensus about any aspect of our very complex lives.

This, ultimately, is what we call knowledge.

INTRODUCTION
THE NUMERICAL FABRIC
OF OUR MODERN LIVES

I've started several different businesses over the course of my career. One was a hedge fund. Our investment strategy focused on the electricity industry, my "domain" for the past thirty-five years. When you launch a hedge fund, you have many meetings with potential investors in metropolitan New York City. One thing I noticed during these meetings: Everyone touted their economic and financial models. Of course, they were proprietary, and we weren't ever allowed to "look under the hood." Our modest fund also used a "model," an econometric model. We were like kids left alone for a play date, one-upping each other about our models. Honestly, the whole time I worked with these money managers, I never really understood what was behind our econometric model. The "model guy" on our staff never really could explain it. He just insisted it was a "pretty good model." I sure was impressed with the graphs and tables the computer spit out, though!

Good models used correctly provide insight into

some phenomenon, evidence to support decisions, a base from which to extrapolate something larger, support for government regulation, for example, or repeal of existing legislation. Models are simplified versions of a process, phenomenon, behavior, or situation designed to lead down the path towards an objective reality.

Good models form the basis for unique new products and services which enhance individual and social well-being. However, in my career, I've learned that the term "model" is often used to scare someone. Ooooh, she has a model, it's bigger and badder than someone else's model. Models are also used to gain a competitive advantage, to advocate for one position over another, and to silence critics with "hard data."

The fundamental flaw with all models is they are designed by humans, and therefore all models carry the natural, unconscious or deliberate biases of their creators and the uses/users they are created for.

Over and over again, I am astonished, shocked even, at how simple a model can be. Sometimes a "model" is an equation, like the ones you learned (or didn't, as the case might be) in algebra. You don't have to know how to do math to remember what an equation is. It's something like $y = ax + b$. It is something you can plot to get a graph, a pretty picture, if you have data for the independent variable (x), and know what the constants are (a, b). You solve for the dependent variable y, in other words.

In one simple form of modeling, the investigator

starts by taking measurements if she has a hypothesis that y is somehow dependent on x. The data is plotted, and the equation which best describes the plot, often called the "best fit," becomes the model.

Before you simply accept the model's results, it is important to ask what constitutes a "measurement?" Another phrase that should cause you to scrunch up your face and raise your eyebrows is "best fit." We will delve into these aspects of numerical analysis later, and as we'll see, the line or plot that "fits best" may still not tell us anything worth knowing, especially if each of the data points, the measurements, are riddled with error and bias.

As mentioned above, models can be ridiculously elementary. They've become part of our lexicon mostly because the computation has been automated. The actual math is often performed in an Excel Spreadsheet, Excel being a standard piece of data and analysis software in Microsoft's Office Suite. People build simple models in Excel and talk about them like they've redefined quantum mechanics. I should know. I'm a consultant. This is one thing consultants do very well.

Here's a good example. You might think that the "oil life" indicator on your car's dashboard is based on a sophisticated algorithm, incorporating a measure of oil cleanliness, time interval between oil changes, engine performance, and so on. It should provide numerical evidence that it's time to change the oil. It should be based on the actual condition of the oil.

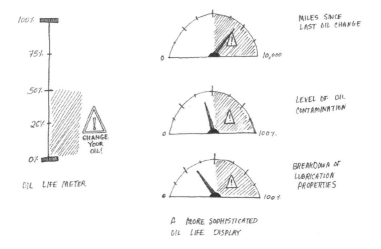

Alas, it simply indicates the number of miles you've driven since the last oil change. But the digital readout and the warning are compelling, aren't they?

The oil life indicator isn't there to minimize the cost and inconvenience of oil changes, to say nothing of responsible disposal of the used oil. It's a dashboard readout designed to make you think twice about going too long before taking the vehicle in for service. It's designed to scare you, not inform you. It's more reminder than indicator. It's there in the service of the dealer or the service shop as much as you, the owner.

Other models can be hopelessly complex (for all but the subject matter specialist). Models used to forecast global climate change are like this. Climatologists have taken computer modeling to infinity and beyond, or least to the outer reaches of the earth's atmosphere.

Economists build and apply complex models to forecast growth, determine fiscal policy, and try (though they almost always fail) to predict the onset of the next recession. Somehow, that repeated failure doesn't deter those who pay economists and other financial engineers big money to tweak their models for "the next time."

Sometimes a financial analyst, economist, or pollster does successfully anticipate the onset of an economic malady, irrational exuberance, or a candidate for elected office. They become the celebrated go-to experts until the same methodology fails to anticipate the next big event.

In this book, I use the term "model" to refer interchangeably to a mathematical model, a computer model, an algorithm, an econometric model, a financial model, a forecasting model, or an equation. A model is any relationship between or among two or variables. Modeling in turn refers to the construction and use of the model. Graphs and plots are then used to explain or simplify what the models are telling us.

Once a model is constructed from the original data, new data, or inputs, are used to calculate new results, or outputs. This is what is meant by "crunching the numbers." The independent variables in a model have to be measured or have assigned values. The dependent variables have to be calculated.

Whether you are comfortable with math or not, don't run the other way when someone pulls a model out of her figurative holster and starts firing it. Rather, commit the forthcoming commandments explained here to memory, then fire back! Quants, people who are comfortable with math and crunch data, use numbers to paint a picture, just like you would use words. And despite people's perceptions of numbers, especially those who should know better, numbers bandied about are often no more accurate, no more objective, than the meanings of many of the words we use.

Getting a point across with numbers, too often, is just a different form of painting or story-telling. It can be artistry. It can be schlock. It can be authentic. It can be a fake. It takes a tremendous amount of effort to make it real art and/or science.

SECTION I

THE TWELVE COMMANDMENTS OF A NUMERICAL SKEPTIC

I. ACKNOWLEDGE ERROR

Error is everywhere. It's like the noxious molecules of pollution in the air we breathe. It's there, but it's mostly invisible. Sometimes we see it. Sometimes we catch a whiff. Usually, we prefer not to dwell on it. We'd rather accentuate the positive, not dwell on the negative.

As explained in the last chapter, data and measurements are used to develop models and models are then used to reflect, explain, depict, or predict some objective reality; extrapolate beyond the original data used to construct the model; and/or provide some insight into physical or human behavior. Every number, every numerical value, measured or calculated for some practical purpose, has potential error associated with it. After all, there is no such thing as perfection. Rarely is something 100 percent accurate. So the errors associated with each datum in the model are propagated throughout the model.

The atomic clock, against which all other measures of time are compared, has a teeny tiny amount of absolute measurement error, but because it is the standard for the world, it is assumed to be perfect, because it is a reference standard. But it is not perfect. It's the most accurate by scientific consensus. The error is said to be one second in over 100 million years. That's about as close to zero as we get in the practical world of science. Yet, the error is there.

Assumed and assumptions are important words as we get into *Painting By Numbers*. An assumption is something taken to be true or correct or fact for the purposes of modeling and analysis. Sometimes an assumption is later proven to be correct. More often, an assumption is a crutch to make the model work. Until an assumption is proven true or correct, it is a potential source of error in the analysis.

Error takes such forms as inaccuracy, imprecision, bias, ignorance, carelessness, and uncertainty. Critically, inherent error should be carried with that value and made visible wherever that value goes next. The sum total of all possible sources of error should be disclosed with every model, every attempt at numerical analysis. This requires discipline and fortitude.

It is just as important to understand what is wrong with our results as what might be right about them. The error may be heavy, but just like our "brother," it's the burden we have to carry (like in The Hollies' song).

Sadly, such disclosure is rare. Error is usually tossed out like fast food wrappers, ignored, kept in a figurative room in the attic. I've always wondered about this. Does error embarrass people? Is perfection so desired? What kind of society are we that we don't discuss error in polite company?

The temperature the weather service gives you for your location isn't 83F; it is 83F +/- some quantifiable error associated with how that number is arrived at. Ambient temperature can be measured very accurately for the purpose of weather reporting. The temperature forecast for twenty-four hours from now, well, that's going to be dependent on a weather model which incorporates how a weather system is moving towards the location, historical trends in daily variations, and other factors.

Some data input to a model are measured directly, some are inferred indirectly, and some may just be assumed. Sometimes a variable doesn't have a measurement in the strict sense of that word, but instead has a "value."

For instance, temperature is a measurement. It is an indicator of heat or cold. It is a physical phenomenon. When you walk outside, and report to someone else, "It's cold!" that's a subjective observation about temperature, but it is not a measurement. Values are not measurements. A polling questionnaire may ask if you are Democrat or Republican, or it may ask you to fill in the blank of your political affiliation. That's a value, not a measurement.

Value and measurements are both subject to errors.

All inputs to a model have error. The error propagates through the model into the results. The error can also be magnified, depending on the complexity of the model. If you measured x many times and then solved an equation for y, the error in your x measurements will appear in y. If your x term is squared (multiplied to itself), your error is squared too. That's how the error gets magnified.

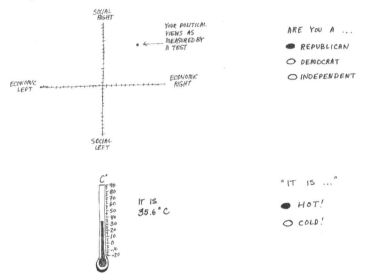

Suppose our model is designed to investigate traits of a group of people in a room. The number of people in the room at a particular time should be a pretty accurate number. It is fixed, unless someone didn't count correctly, or the definition of "people" changes. Or a few people are in the restroom at the time of counting. Just getting counts in a room to match among several counters can be trying if it's a large number. We can probably agree, though, that it is at least a number with low relative risk for error.

Most numbers used in models are not numbers with low relative risk for error. Error analysis is the method(s) by which you determine how the errors of the inputs/data are carried through the "model" into the results. It is a technical subject unto itself. Most everyone who performs modeling and data analysis, whether engineer or social scientist, is required to take courses in understanding error and model limitations.

As I mentioned earlier, I learned error analysis as part of my lab courses in engineering school. Decades later, I took a class in statistical analysis and methods as part of my graduate work in sociology. Many of us are taught about error in some way. We just tend to ignore it, or defer the discussion to others. Even most experts leave error analysis out of their work unless they are hanging out with other experts. When it is included, it's often at such a basic level as to be almost meaningless.

An election poll is a classic example—the results will usually state "within +/- 3 margin of error." Everyone jumps for joy. Candidate A is in the lead! Candidate B is within the margin of error! We're all winners here!

All that "margin" refers to is statistical error. That's only one source of error. All the others, such as how the questions were phrased, what order the questions were asked, how the sample size and sample subjects were developed, what assumptions are implicit in the model, are not revealed or discussed.

If you asked 500 people to check a box indicating

whether they are Democrat or Republican, and then surveyed 500 others with a blank to fill in regarding political affiliation, how different do you suppose the results would be? Chances are, many would see their political affiliation as something different from Democrat or Republican. They might write conservative, or liberal, or progressive. Just because you are registered with one party doesn't mean you always vote that party's candidate. It may not even mean you agree with much of its platform and policies. Pollsters, like many others in a competitive economy, like to think of their modeling and numerical analysis as "black arts," leaving most of us wondering what proprietary secrets are hidden under the hood.

Step onto a scale. The weight indicated has error associated with it. Weight is, among other things, dependent on elevation. Every scale makes an assumption of a constant elevation, such as sea level. It might seem more accurate if it's a digital readout and not numbers with dashes in between them and a line where your weight falls (or the antiquated hunk of iron in your doctor's office). But it's not necessarily more accurate.

I weigh myself every Saturday after my workout in order to determine whether or not I can eat a slice(s) of pie for desert over the weekend. Then I go to the doctor and am shocked that the weight at the doctor's office is higher than my series of weights recorded at home. I just weighed myself on a scale at my parents' house, and it gave a reading almost two pounds more than I was expecting. Is that instrument error? Did I gain two pounds eating mom's cooking? Is it because my parents live at a different elevation? Which scale is more accurate? I need to know because pie is at stake!

While the scale's readout has inherent error associated with it, it's probably accurate enough for the purposes for which it was designed. Still, people obsessed with their weight, accomplished dieters, etc., learn ways to manipulate their weight as indicated on a scale. I'll ruin my chances of having a great weigh in on Saturday morning after my work out if I snarf down pizza Friday evening. All that salt makes me retain water I can't sweat out. I can also "fudge" in the other direction by eating a very light meal Friday evening. It's easy to influence the weight you record tomorrow by what and how much you eat today. It's easy to tweak the objective reality of your weight. Boxers and jockeys used to do it all the time. Maybe they still do.

There are at least three types of error associated with my weight: The inherent error in the measuring device (the scale) and the error I fudged in from my own human biases are two. If I actually recorded these figures every Saturday, there could be potential recording error—I might make a mistake writing down a value. In later chapters, we'll spend plenty of quality time on human biases, because while you might see mention of statistical or measurement error, you hardly ever see the litany of human biases around data and numerical results.

Weight is one simple numerical measurement we all are used to that has at least three sources of error associated with it. The same was true of the +/-3 error band reported with election forecast. Only one type of error is typically "carried" with the results.

Regardless of how heavy, error has to be carried, acknowledged, and embraced like a brother or sister.

It ain't heavy, it's my error.

Statistical and measurement errors, such as the error typically reported with polling and associated with a scale, have nothing to do with human biases. Bias, even though it's proven by psychologists, sociologists, and every other expert and non-expert to exist, is less visible.

Here's a bias that is particularly relevant. We tend to confirm our previous actions rather than contradict them. If we invest in a product, for example, we have a bias towards being satisfied with that product rather than admit we made a mistake. We want to confirm our previous actions and decisions. This is confirmation bias.

Confirmation bias is being blamed for the inaccurate polling which took place during the recent presidential election. Actually, it wasn't so much that the polling was inaccurate as the reporting on the polling incomplete. Some polling models purported to be more accurate because they were a "poll of polls." That means they take the results from all the polls and analyze them together. This technique can indeed provide higher accuracy. It can also magnify the inherent error, especially if all of the sub-polls are biased in the same direction!

I have a friend who recommends every movie he goes to. If he went and enjoyed it, it must be good enough for his friends. He is imposing confirmation bias on his recommendations; he isn't considering his friends' interests and movie tastes, only his own.

Here's another form of bias: We tend to select based on our own traits. Most of us will choose to live in a neighborhood of people much like us socio-economically, or congregate in social networks with the like-minded. This is called self-selection bias.

Here's a third: Most people prefer to say something good or not say anything at all, as that parental admonition goes. We have a predilection to accentuate the positive. Okay, there are a few dark-cloud types out there. For instance, me, for writing this book.

Health and medical studies are always imperiled by the healthy user bias. Someone who is healthy is going to show a beneficial result of eating or behaving in a certain way just because they are already healthy.

There are sources of error and inherent biases. Some are deliberate. Some are unwitting. But all have to be identified, accounted for, and carried with the results. Recognizing that all numbers have error, or at least potential error, is the first step. The second is recognizing that all models require assumptions, the subject of the second commandment.

2. IDENTIFY ASSUMPTIONS

As mentioned in the introduction, assumptions are necessary parts of modeling and numerical analysis. One type of assumption is something taken to be true or correct until it is actually shown to be correct (or, conversely, shown to be false and discarded—or not). Other assumptions are required to make the model work. A modeler might hypothesize that one thing is dependent on another, until data analysis proves that to be correct or incorrect. A modeler might also assume something is normal, or historical, like weather patterns.

Some assumptions are good, some are not so good. Some are good at the time, but are shown to be not good at some future point in time. Assuming a normal weather pattern works until a weather event occurs that upsets the definition of "normal." Assuming a "normal" election pattern works until an election occurs that is a complete anomaly. Assuming "historical" home buying patterns is fine for selling financial products based on home mortgages until homes stop selling and no one really knows why.

Or at least no one knows why at the time.

Assumptions are necessary because the principal objective of a model is to simplify what the model is designed to represent for the purposes of achieving an output and offering insight. That's why a poll or survey is based on a sample that is supposed to adequately, hopefully even accurately, reflect the larger population or system being studied.

When you build a physical model of an object, it's often described as at a scale of 1:10 or 1:100. I recall when engineers built a scale model of an entire refinery or powerplant to guide the construction of the actual facility. It's a great tool for visualizing interferences, gauging dimensional issues, and generally anticipating how everything will fit together. (Today these models are often built using computer aided design, or CAD programs, rather than physically.) But in most cases, such a complete model doesn't include every valve, pipe, instrument, and object. It's a simplified representation for specific purposes. It's not meant for purposes it was not designed. While that may sound like a truism, you'd be surprised at how often it is violated.

Mathematical models, like physical models, are designed to simplify a real situation for a specific purpose. To do this, they always need assumptions, characteristics about the model that are assumed to be true, or constant, or "good enough," regardless of whether they actually are. Models used in physics and chemistry and engineering and biology, or the "hard sciences," are often based on "ideal" situations. These ideal situations don't exist in the real world, but even if they only exist as theoretical constructs, they are still useful because they give us a theoretical limit. They offer boundaries within which we can study practical applications.

Boyle's law governing the relationship between temperature, pressure, volume, and density of a gas assumes that the gas exists in an "ideal state." This ideal state does not exist in the real world, even if it can be approached in a laboratory. Yet Boyle's law has proven immensely useful for close to two centuries. In the real world, it is applied with "correction" factors. It's a model of the physical world.

Most econometric models (which reflect economic activity based on measured inputs, or metrics) assume that consumers act "rationally." That's an ideal situation, just like Boyle's law. But consumers don't act rationally at all. Who is even to say what is and isn't "rational?" Economists can argue this point all day long. Nevertheless, the rational economic actor is what most macro-economic models revolve around.

A model used to study beach erosion might assume that waves hitting the shore are of a constant force for a certain number of hours a day, or it may assume that the impacted beach always has the same dimensions, grade, sand texture, etc. I remember as a kid at summer camp playing on the beach at Chesapeake Bay and getting sand castles ready for when the big ocean-liners passed on the horizon. That's because my campmates and I knew the waves induced by the ships would be much bigger and crash our castles when they reached shore. The force of crashing waves is not constant, but a model might require such an assumption.

Assumptions often lead to gross simplifications of a real situation and, therefore, are by definition sources of error. An election season poll "model" might assume (that troubling word again) that people who have cell phones are the same as people who don't, or that people active on social media are the same as people who aren't. An on-line poll might not adequately take into account avatars, or people pretending to be someone else. These have been shown in past elections to be poor assumptions, and the models proven inadequate, occasionally resulting in really bad predictions propagated throughout the media. Election cycle after election cycle, these poor assumptions are aired incessantly, but suitable improvements to them are still lacking.

Models wouldn't exist without assumptions, but they can be dangerous unless they are recognized and acknowledged. People who construct and profit from models usually hope people consider the model as a whole, as a black box, and the predictions they make are too often elevated to what some consider as mysterious and compelling as any "black art." Like magic, in other words. Like a supplicant seeking wisdom at the Delphic

Oracle in ancient Greece, you are expected to believe even if you don't understand what the Oracle is babbling on about and need the high priests in the temple (modern day model makers, statisticians, and mathematicians) to interpret the Oracle's pronouncements.

Don't simply trust. Don't simply believe. Instead deconstruct the model. When you do that, you will find something taken for granted or something taken as constant that isn't, or as a truism that is not (like rational economics man). It may be a useful assumption in certain situations but certainly not in all or even many situations.

Along with those assumptions, you may find approximations. Sometimes they are good ones, sometimes not.

"Assuming" an average rate of inflation over a fifty year economic event horizon probably isn't a bad assumption; over a five year period, it could be disastrous. Assuming an average height for a male or female in one country may not be prudent in another because of different dietary and labor habits, etc.

Unfortunately, identifying assumptions and approximations is like pulling teeth. It requires that the modeler, the person using (or paying for) the model, and everyone else affected by the model admit to its limitations, rather than laud the results it has achieved as revealed wisdom.

If you quiz modelers about their assumptions, I can almost guarantee you will find something a little suspicious. Often, the suspect assumption will be the "weakest link" and unfortunately, as we'll see in the next chapter, the model is only as strong as its weakest link.

3. FIND THE WEAKEST LINK

Error in models is worse than the bathtub ring in *The Cat in the Hat Comes Back*. Not only can't you get rid of error, it propagates and magnifies. A poor assumption can be a grave error in a model that never goes away. Similarly, a measurement with a high degree of error associated with it is carried through the model to the results. That's why numerical results are only as strong as the most error-prone link in the model. It seems obvious, but it is easy to ignore or forget.

Let's consider weak links with the example of body mass index, or BMI. It has a pretty simple equation and model. When I step on my scale at home (after a good workout!), it reads 169 pounds. I am 5 ft, 9 in. tall. I do the requisite calculation.

BMI = Weight (kilograms)/height^2 (meters)

For those of us who live under a government that refuses to use the measurement system of the rest of the world, BMI = 0.45 weight (lbs)/[height (inches) x 2.54 (cm/in) x m/100 cm]^2.

My result is 24.7. When I step on the scale at any doctor's office, I am always around ten pounds heavier than what my scale at home reads. If I use the doc's reading, my BMI is 26.2. There is a 1.5 difference between the two, or 6 percent.

Fortunately, whatever I might do with my BMI index probably does not require accuracy better than this. What others might do with my BMI figure may be different.

We can know weight and height with a high degree of accuracy. So BMI should be a pretty accurate metric, one with low relative risk of error. But suppose I want to comfort myself that I am not "overweight." That difference caused by scale measurement error could loom large.

In fact, it does! That's why I use this example. The range for a "healthy" BMI is 19-25. It has always bothered the hell out of me that, despite all my exercising and careful eating, I am on the threshold of unhealthy. So what? I know better. I can get past this. And besides, isn't "healthy" subjective? It's only a number, after all, and I'm not far off. But I am a numbers kind of guy, and the reality is BMI has become an accepted "standard" of sorts for health related to obesity.

It could be worse. Suppose my insurance provider offers discounts for "healthy" drivers? Could I lose my discount if I am now categorized as unhealthy and "overweight?" What if a condition of a specific employment opportunity is that I am not overweight? I could be on the threshold of a bad judgment all because a doctor's scale shows me ten pounds heavier than I thought I was.

Luckily those scenarios do not apply to me, and I can comfort myself that I am not overweight by simply using the measurement from my scale at home.

Error has more egregious impact on results depending on the equations used in the model. In math, there is something called an exponent. When a value is squared (exponent 2) or cubed (exponent 3), it is multiplied by itself that many times. This is what people mean when they talk about exponential growth or change. The number can get big in a hurry.

In the BMI calculation, height is the squared term. Thank goodness! Height propagates much less inaccuracy than weight. A ten-pound difference in my weight as a squared term would really make my BMI look bad. Weight is the weak link in this numerical chain.

A big error in an original measurement or an inferred value just leads to a highly incorrect result. It is when results based on big errors are combined with human judgments that things can spiral out of control.

Just for fun, let's build a simple visual model for BMI. Let's say there are five body types. Each can be represented by a geometric shape. Each shaped is assigned a BMI based on the dimensions of the shape. Spheres (short, fat, and rotund in the middle) are x, tall rectangles (string bean, or tall and lanky) are y, short rectangles (short and stocky) are z, and so on.

Pretend I'm a drill sergeant and I'm going to eyeball all of my new recruits in boot camp and assign them one of these five body types with an associated BMI. My superior officer then is going to take the data and report them to headquarters. Headquarters is then going to aggregate the data to determine trends in the BMI of recruits.

You can imagine how much error is inherent in this crude modeling exercise. You're probably scoffing. It's a silly example because it's pretty straightforward to obtain height and weight data for recruits, and calculate accurate BMI.

But let's consider this same thought process for a very serious situation. Let's say you constructed a model for how water flows through and around a landfill and subsequently how that water might reach aquifers, freshwater lakes, streams, etc. Academic modeling experts are pressed into service for this type of situation. The models developed can have simplifying factors as bad or worse than the BMI shapes I posit above.

Let's further assume that the model is then applied to hundreds of landfills around the country in different geographic areas with very different geological characteristics. Then the results of these landfill modeling studies are aggregated to show that, on a national basis, groundwater contamination from landfills is rampant.

You can probably see how the errors could propagate, and, in fact, this is what happens when a standard, accepted model is used, and then abused, because it is applied to situations it was not designed for and supporting purposes for which it was never intended. The model itself becomes the weak link in the numerical chain. But policy-makers use such aggregated data from models like this to conclude that something must be done about groundwater contamination by landfills. This "something" becomes a regulatory requirement to construct barriers, install liners between the waste volume and the soil, collect and treat water runoff around the landfill, and otherwise substantially raise the expenses of landfilling waste.

In no way am I arguing that it's a bad idea to protect groundwater from wastes or institute such regulations. In no way do I want this to serve as an example of science denial (or more aptly, engineering denial). What I do want you to consider, though, is how inherent modeling errors propagate through "systems"—the landfill modeling expert system, the regulatory system, the consumer disposal system, and the economic system. If a bad model is used to determine the extent of groundwater contamination, it really can potentially affect the entire economy!

Was such a landfill water runoff model developed to accurately evaluate the impact of water runoff on freshwater supply? Or was it developed to advocate for stricter environmental management policies? Or, conversely, could a similar model be constructed by landfill management companies using different assumptions, approximations, and measurements? Of course. And those on different sides of environmental policy vehemently pose these questions, usually as accusations, all the time.

Errors which may (or may not have been) inherent to that model are now part and parcel of a regulatory framework that governs every landfill in the country. If you favor greater environmental regulation, you probably don't care. If you favor less regulation to business, you probably do.

Let's take the type of situation I have faced in my consulting practice. I have to evaluate the prospects for a new technology replacing a current option. The horizon over which I must judge this is twenty years.

Two of the most important inputs to my evaluation are the future prices for natural gas and electricity. Over the last ten years, natural gas prices have fluctuated between $2/million Btu and $14/million Btu, with little regional variability. That is quite a spread. However, for most of that time, it has been between $2.50/million Btu and $5/million Btu.

You can see how the range I select over the coming 20-year period will influence the outcome. In most evaluations in my consulting world, the assumptions about future energy commodity prices are usually the weak link in the numerical chain, especially electricity prices.

Electricity prices fluctuate daily, weekly, seasonally, and regionally. In the course of a really hot day, electricity prices might fluctuate by an order of magnitude. On some days of the year, prices can fluctuate by one hundred times at least a few hours of the day.

Forecasting average electricity prices over twenty years is one thing. But what if this new technology is intended to exploit very extreme spreads within individual days or even hours? I have to make what amounts to an educated guess that, for a certain number of hours over that twenty-year period, this technology will make my client enough money to pay back the investment. I will make this educated guess by modeling with reams of historical electricity pricing data.

Consultants make good money evaluating the economic efficacy of engineered systems based on past economic data. But mostly what they are doing is giving an opinion supported by a model that spits out a numerical narrative which can be used to argue with other stakeholders against alternative numerical narratives. By the time the winning narrative gets to the executive suite, the story is being told with colorful graphs and tables.

In my experience, most modeling conducted today is for advocacy support, not necessarily to approach an inherent objective reality. But we now know models are only as good as their weakest links. Models can be brilliant confirming the past, but not much better than guesswork for forecasting the future. In other words, past performance is no guarantee of future results, the subject of our next commandment.

4. SEPARATE PAST PERFORMANCE FROM FUTURE RESULTS

Stock brokers, mutual fund managers, and investment advisors are obligated to repeat to customers, usually in the fine print: Past performance is no guarantee of future results.

This statement should be carved into all our foreheads so we see it every time we look in the mirror. That's because many models are designed to forecast something about the future, but let's face it, the future is unknowable. We only guess based on past experience.

The general sequence of steps in modeling goes like this:

A theoretical model is conceived to represent a specific situation, whether that situation is global climate change, water flow through a landfill, stock market performance, future price of bonds, value of an electricity grid technology, sales of product, change in BMI as people age, effect of a new drug on a group of subjects suffering from an illness, or myriad other situations.

After the theoretical model—the mathematical

relationship between the inputs and the outputs—is established, the model is "calibrated" with actual data.

Taking the calibration a step further is called model validation. The model has to show it can output a result that is already known to be true, or has been previously recorded. In this regard, a model is often "back-tested," that is, the model is run to see if it predicts an actual result from historical data.

Finally, the model is "adjusted" to fit more data and situations and scenarios. Repeat: The model is adjusted to fit the data. This is where lots of problems occur.

A model applied to a situation with little variability in inputs can work surprisingly well over a long period of time (years) and large data sets. The more a model is able to output results which are known, or which come true in the future, the more confidence everyone has in the model.

Importantly, when data changes appreciably, the model no longer functions as well. It has to be re-calibrated. In many instances, you need to throw out the old model and construct a new one. Most modelers resist this.

Some models have been proven over time to work wonderfully. The Carnot cycle is a theoretical model developed in the 1800s to describe how heat engines perform. To this day, it is used as a basis for building and automating energy systems. It is such a good model that it is called a "first principles" model—the principles being those of thermodynamics. For our purposes (though not perhaps at the quantum level or throughout the universe), thermodynamics embodies irrefutable laws of physics.

Another way a model gets better is with huge amounts of data. Engineers today can predict with high probability approximately when a machine will fail by crunching a huge amount of operating data about that machine and machines like it doing similar things around the world. The models detect patterns of behavior in the machine. These patterns can be extrapolated into the near future.

Suppose you are reviewing three measurements taken on a machine. The values are the same or similar to the measurements recorded a year ago when the machine failed and two years ago when the machine had a kink which had to be repaired. This is called pattern recognition. An operator is alerted that something bad may be about to happen with this machine whenever those three measurements are similar at the same time.

This type of modeling tends to work pretty well because such machines are replicas of each other. The variations among them tend to be very small, at least coming out of the factory. Their "future performance" isn't likely to deviate much from their "past" performance.

You can take reams and reams of operating data and then analyze that data for telltale patterns of wear, failure precursors, and other performance factors. However, as these machines age and operate year after year after year and, perhaps, under different conditions, the variations among them get larger and such modeling isn't as effective. This is why data scientists often say that every machine in time becomes its own unique entity from a data perspective.

Think of your car. Thousands of people drive the same model car you have. But some people drive it on tropical islands with extreme humidity and temperature and blowing sand; others drive in northern latitudes with low temperatures and frequent freezing conditions. Some drive in cities with paved roads, some drive in the country on gravel or dirt roads. Some of those cars are rented out by rental agencies and therefore have been driven by many drivers each with their peculiar driving habits.

Variations in those cars one month after leaving the dealership are small, perhaps even insignificant. After months and years with different drivers in different locations on different types of surfaces with different maintenance regimes, the variability will begin to challenge any "model" created by the manufacturer to forecast future performance, set maintenance schedules, etc.

On the flip side, with enough historical performance and operating data, an "operating model" of any machine can be continually updated to describe its unique characteristics. Your car doesn't have enough value to pay for such models. The power plant or paper mill or computer chip manufacturing plant, however, can benefit from investment in such models. Past performance of machines used in these facilities can be pretty good indicators of future performance.

A very complex global climate model also gets better with huge data sets of temperature, humidity, wind patterns, catastrophic events, and so on from all around the world. One problem with global climate models is the accuracy of inputs which describe past climate behavior and climate states.

The fact is, climate modelers use proxies to infer conclusions about planetary warming and cooling. A proxy is a measurement used to infer something about a variable which can't be measured. A good example: Tree rings of a stump are used to infer the age of a tree. A more complicated example: carbon levels in the atmosphere millions of years ago, which obviously weren't measured and recorded, are inferred from greenhouse gas concentrations in arctic ice cores.

Cave men didn't leave records about temperature, wind speed, and whether it was a "dry heat" that day. Don't take this as climate denial, but instead realize that proxy measurements are necessary for complex models to work.

And speaking of proxy measurements, imagine forecasting beer sales by watching the temperature gauge. Thanks to a corporate data scientist who reviewed a draft of this manuscript, I learned that beer sales are apparently dependent on temperature and precipitation. Beverage companies use models to explain variances in sales when temperatures are above or below "normal." During an abnormally hot spring in 2012, one beer maker experienced skyrocketing sales and scrambled to keep up. Since that data had never been modeled before, that "new territory" for sales could not be anticipated by the model. According to this data expert for said beer company, "our models always assume normal weather, but weather is never normal."

Most of the pollsters are probably saying something similar about the last presidential campaign.

This leads to another saying worthy of imprint on our foreheads: Models can be effective at explaining something that has already happened, but not so good at predicting something that hasn't happened.

Let's look at stock market performance. How do you predict when irrational collective behavior overtakes individual common sense, when people rush to the bank in a panic instead of sitting patiently at home watching their money grow through compound interest?

The answer is you can't. But that doesn't prevent lots of experts getting paid huge salaries to pretend they can. Some of this divining of the future may be considered "independent research" but most of it really is advocacy for something (A) over something else (B). Professionals who trade in precious metals, for example, rarely forecast great things for the economy. That's because precious metals, like land, are regarded as investments of last resort (A), when everything else (B) goes to hell in a handbasket.

Models for metals investing tend to forecast doomsday scenarios, all day every day. Models for public stocks tend to be the opposite.

Should anyone believe the revenue forecasts in the five year plan of a new smart phone digital app company? Most of these companies haven't even been in business for five years. They don't even have past performance! Yet people with lots of burnable cash don't think twice when it comes to investing in venture-type tech companies who wave their five year plan (complete with lots of colorful charts and graphs) next to the company flag.

The fact is, models can only be validated with historical data or by predicting something that does come true, or is already known. But while the immediate past tends to resemble the immediate future, the past is not a prelude to the future. Some models don't even predict the past very well.

The lower the variability in the data over time compared to the historical data used to calibrate and validate it, the better the model will "guarantee" future performance. I might plan tomorrow based on what today was like, but not next year.

Past performance is no guarantee of future results. It's a shame, really, that only investment specialists are forced to carry this in the fine print.

One thing's for sure: If you can't convince someone that you've divined the future with lots of numbers and analysis, then draw them a picture (or make colorful charts and graphs)!

5. QUESTION THE PICTURE

I've always been obsessed with the conversion of words to numbers to words. After all, that is the foundation of how I've made a living for almost four decades as an engineer who loved to write, an engineering and technology journalist, and as an industry consultant.

But I've always been, shall we say (and this is being generous), graphically challenged. Lots of people are the opposite. They'd rather get the pictorial version of the story. Today, there's an army of "data artists" who make really interesting pictures like heat maps from data.

To explain numbers today, you need words and pictures. Let's take some time to understand these conversion processes.

Election season polls are a good first example. A news organization, which prides itself on independent journalism, conducts regular polls for a state primary. The objective, ostensibly, is to offer the viewer/reader an "objective" view of who is most likely to win, or who is currently in the lead.

Here is the breakdown of what happens:

- A random sample of subjects reflecting the population in the aggregate being studied, is generated
- A questionnaire is developed
- A survey is taken over phone or in person
- Results are tabulated and analyzed
- The results are extrapolated from the sample to the population at large
- Graphs and tables are drawn to make the results easier to digest and understand
- News outlets report the results

The pollster's questions are constructed from words. The responses to the words are converted into numbers. The numbers are converted into pictures. The numbers and pictures are then converted into another set of words reported to audiences, usually with the most dramatic pictures.

Nothing can go wrong, right? Ever listen to three eye witnesses give their accounts of what happened at a crime scene? Or siblings recall an event on a vacation years earlier, or even a conversation from dinner the night before?

Consider a medical trial. The objective is to determine if fictitious new drug, MEDTRIP A, has a beneficial effect on cognitive processes. Here are some of the steps in the validation protocol:

- A group of subjects is established with similar cognitive ability.
- A control group of subjects is established who are given a placebo, essentially tricked into believing they are also being administered MEDTRIP A.
- The remaining subjects are given MEDTRIP A for a period of time.
- Change in cognitive function is measured for both groups.
- Change in cognitive function is measured by both sensory measurement of brain function, tests of the subjects brain function, and questions posed to each subject.
- Differences are analyzed, quantified, and reported in an academic journal, usually with illustrations.

Nothing can go wrong, right? Maybe the better question is, how much can go right?

The greatest problem with medical testing, just like polling, is the experts involved in the protocol (scientists, regulators, etc.) are focused on the statistical error in the sample. What about the baseline definition of cognitive ability, how the questions to the subjects are phrased, and how the measurements are made?

A common challenge to both polling and medical testing is the all-important representative sample. That's important for statistical validity. Another, specific to this case, is an accepted baseline level of cognitive ability, some standard. If one doesn't exist, you need to go and create one, perhaps with other pharma companies.

One large source of error, regardless of the situation being studied, is the fact that people tend to behave differently when they are being observed. In other words, the very act of measuring, observing, and paying attention changes the subject's behavior and responses. This is a well-proven phenomenon backed by decades of psychological research. (Interestingly, a similar "observer effect" exists in physics and refers to changes that the very act of observation make on the phenomenon being observed.)

Now consider how sources of error are propagated from step to step. First, realize that MEDTRIP A may not have progressed to human testing without prior testing on animals. Animals, of course, may also be biological beings with similarities to humans, but they are not humans. We're not even going to get into the potential for error caused by that "minor" discrepancy. When tens of millions of dollars are being spent on new pharmaceuticals, there is not only measurement and statistical error inherent to the testing and validation process; there is human bias built in to move towards a successful result as quickly as possible (despite that drug testing takes many years, decades even), a result that will pay back the company's investment in the research and development around MEDTRIP A.

It may sound cynical, but this source of collective bias filtering down to each participant on the MEDTRIP testing and launch team has to be factored in. Human bias, like all error, can't be eliminated. It can only be minimized. But first it must be recognized.

Every positive result or observation tends to be amplified as the long process of drug validation and approval moves forward. This inherent bias also is amplified as the narrative representation of the experiment design is translated into numerical values and analysis and then converted into a different narrative to explain the results—to regulators, doctors, and health insurers.

Accentuating the positive often means amplifying the errors, because the negative is being ignored. The next time you watch a television commercial for a new pharmaceutical drug, observe the difference between the behavior of the actors and the dangers promulgated in the fine print language being read. One is the picture. The other is the words. The picture accentuates the positive. I would argue that the picture is expressly designed to deflect attention from the negatives.

Remember my example in the preface, me the high school senior applying a numerical model to select a college? I caught myself intentionally biasing the results towards a school I had already selected in my mind. In fact, I was applying the model to satisfy my father, and bias the result towards the school I had already decided on, not to improve my chances for selecting the "right" school for me.

Bias is a dangerous undercurrent. In an organization which must achieve certain results to survive, it can be insidious, regardless of what protocols are established to guard against it. From my experience, I can't overemphasize this point. I've observed whole new technologies develop over a period of several decades, and most of them have what I call an Achilles heel, a technical shortcoming which never actually goes away. It's never engineered out of the system. This shortcoming usually comes back to haunt the companies who sell product based on the technology and the buyers who deploy the product.

One good example is a fuel cell, a device that makes electricity and heat from fuel far more efficiently than most "engines." Every fuel cell has something called a membrane through which some molecules flow (and others don't). The operating life of this membrane has been an "Achilles heel" of fuel cell technology as it was scaled up from laboratory versions to commercial products, and a collective avoidance of overcoming the limitations of this membrane developed. There may be good reasons for this—cost, optimization, etc.—that cause an inadequate membrane to be something everyone just accepts, but still, the limitation has been propagated through the development process.

The greatest source of bias is how graphics and visuals are made, which illustrations are selected, and how the pictures shape the narrative and slant the story. It capitalizes on a universal human weakness to notice the pictures first, and deal with all the rest of it later. Rely on visual capacity first!

I accompanied my ninety-two year old father to his regular neurologist appointment. We were surrounded by all the freebies and giveaways for a new cognition drug in the waiting room. I read about the same cognition drug in a magazine while we waited. Lo and behold, the doctor prescribed this new cognition drug after seeing my father, asking him to respond to a few questions, and listening to my assessment of his condition.

The "pictures" and words represent thousands of numbers from R&D and clinical trials, but ultimately they represent what the medical community wants me to know about this drug before it had been prescribed. We had been "pre-conditioned" for the sale.

The business model of a pharmaceutical company is to sell more drugs, even though they must do it with painstaking research, onerous regulatory restrictions, and inordinately expensive manufacturing facilities.

Car companies sell cars. Fuel cell manufacturers sell fuel cells. Drug companies sell drugs. No matter what the end product is, the mathematical models are always in the service of the business model, the subject of the next chapter.

6. UNDERSTAND THE BUSINESS MODEL

I spend much quality consulting time refreshing my client's collective memory about business models. I try to keep it as simple as possible. Numerical models are developed and deployed to service the business model. For that reason, the business model is an important source of error and bias in numerical analysis and modeling.

It's also important not to confuse the business model with an organization's vision statement. The vision or mission statement is an articulation of what the organization strives to do, the ideals they are trying to reach. The business model is how the organization is going to make money, pay its employees, earn a profit, reward shareholders, or satisfy stakeholders.

The business model for a pharmaceutical company is to create new drugs which can earn a profit over and above the investment in research and development and other costs. The vision statement may include things like "enriching the lives and welfare and health of customers."

Companies are organizations of human individuals working to further the goals of the company business model and vision. Universities are collections of individuals organized to achieve the goals of the university. Non-profits are organizations working under different financial and, often, humanitarian goals.

All of them operate with a vision and a business model.

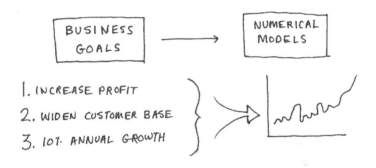

The vision statement of a university may be "to inspire, motivate, educate, and train students for a professional career in public or private service." The business model may require that undergraduate programs be subsidized through graduate research programs and grants as well as high-profile sports programs like football because tuition can't be raised high enough to cover all costs of educating undergrads. Without implementing the business model, the school cannot compete against its peers for new students and cannot fulfill its mission.

The vision of a professor may be to inspire and educate students. The business model of the same professor may be to publish or perish (or get grant funding). The goal of her department might be to remain relevant with respect to educating students and to prove its importance (or value) vis a vis other departments as they compete for funding from the administration.

The business model of a private equity or hedge fund is to pool investor funds, pursue a differentiated investment strategy, distribute gains to the investors, and compensate the firm's partners through fees based on those gains and the total funds under management. Or simply, it is to make money off other people's money by investing it better than each investor can do alone.

Numerical models are used by an organization in the service of the business model. The university has to secure more research grants from private and public sources. The private equity firm has to attract more investors and replace those who leave the fund. The pharma company has to get doctors to prescribe their products for what ails their patients.

Consider how this can impact the use of models. The private equity firm needs a model that shows how its investment strategy is differentiated from its competition. That type of model may be different from normal econometric or financial models. The pharma company is interested in models which convince doctors to write prescriptions for their products. The university is interested in models which show value for research compared to other universities.

Note that these goals don't necessarily require an accurate numerical model, just one that achieves the stated objective. Often, the idea is to manufacture the organization's version of reality rather than find an "objective" reality. This is similar to the use of numerical models in advocacy, but taken to a new level.

The university isn't appealing to undergraduate students with their models (that is done through reputation management, tuition price points, location, sparkling new student centers, new housing and other student benefits, etc.). The pharma company isn't using models that are necessarily going to be understood by patients (unless they are very engaged in their own health maintenance and adore quantitative analysis). And the private equity firm isn't seeking some objective reality and capability to forecast market swings in a volatile sector. In all three cases, the modeling objective is more than advocacy—it is to drive revenue consistent with the business model.

Here's what isn't as obvious: The numerical models used by each in the service of the firm's business model may not necessarily be aligned with the business objectives as understood by customers and other stakeholders outside the organization.

If the private equity fund tanks, the pharmaceutical hurts people instead of helping them, and the university produces undergrads who don't get hired or earn diplomas, they won't stay in business. No amount of modeling overcomes failed performance.

But the pharma company doesn't have to worry too much about patients who buy and use their products who and don't get hurt. As long as they think the drug is helping, that's what matters. As the saying goes, "Do no harm," leaving the issue of neutral outcomes somewhat ambiguous.

For example, the more doctors who "see" (read, view, discuss with peers) that MEDTRIP A is effective, the more it will be prescribed. The notion that doctors are less fallible, less prone to the less savory aspects of the human condition, is naïve. They have their own biases and personal business models. Like all of us, they can be influenced. Studies repeatedly show this to be the case. There is a reason why many times when you wait in a doctor's office, pharma sales reps show up waiting for their appointment with the doc. It's also why regulatory changes have been instituted to reduce the influence of pharma sales staff on doctors (and why so much drug advertising is now targeted directly to patients).

In truth, the "customers" for MEDTRIP A, patients with dementia, are secondary stakeholders in the drug development and approval process. Regulators, insurance companies, and doctors are the primary stakeholders. You can bet that the numerical models deployed in the service of the business model are biased towards the primary stakeholders, not patients.

Again, it's not that pharmaceutical companies, hedge funds, and universities are doing bad things with their models. What's important is transparency in how they are used and for which purposes.

In an election, the goal of the campaign managers is not just to propagate the policy ideas of the candidate they work for but to create doubt about the other candidates ("going negative"). If you can generate a valid poll showing that the leading candidate is slipping one week before the vote, that result can then be propagated through the media. Depending on how the talking heads spin the story about the numbers, the result can start snowballing and soon the poll results are influencing subsequent poll results which influence actual votes.

The business model of a campaign is to get your guy elected without running afoul of the elections rules, not achieve some reflection of objective reality.

If you don't understand the business model, you are destined to be the convenient victim for all those wielding their math models.

Instructive here is the book (and movie) *The Big Short*. It tells the story of those involved in the financial shenanigans around home mortgages which tanked the American economy in 2007 (and the global economy shortly thereafter). A few "geniuses" recognized the saturation in mortgages and flaws in the models used by the big banks backing the collateralized debt obligations (CDOs) they sold to unwitting investors. The big bank models showed how attractive the future value of these CDOs would be to eager investors. Ratings agencies also used their own in-house models to "rate" these investments as great, good, not so good, poor, etc. Since the purveyors of the CDOs pay the ratings agencies for the rating (nope, no conflict of interest here), you can probably see how their valuation models are "aligned" with their business model.

The geniuses made tens of millions of dollars using their own models to exploit the flaws in others' models and then went and got primary source data by visiting areas where homes were being built but no one was buying them.

These geniuses weren't "good guys." They didn't run to the media to report on fraudulent practices. They used their own models to understand when and how the CDOs would crash, "shorting" their investments in these instruments, or betting that their value would decline rather than rise, hence the name of the book and movie. They almost went broke first, too.

That was their differentiated business model.

So, is a university's business model aligned with undergraduate student education? Are the pharmaceutical validation models aligned with the needs of patients? Are the CDO valuation models aligned with the fiduciary interests of big bank customers? You won't know unless you assess the models.

Modeling is a skill, a highly prized and well paid skill. People pay for modeling to support their business model. With that in mind, the numerical model often doesn't have to be necessarily any good and the narrative it tells doesn't have to be right; it just has to further the objectives of the business.

And if you are convinced of how difficult it is to model things like the economy, global climate change, or the market for collateralized debt obligations, just wait for the next chapter when we tackle things which are really difficult to measure: human emotions and feelings.

7. DON'T CONFUSE FEELINGS WITH MEASUREMENTS

Many models are designed to tell us something about how things may change in the future. The "Catch-22" (named after Joseph Heller's classic World War II novel by the same name) is that the more those things change, the harder they are to model. The anti-Catch-22, or the reverse of this, is that the more predictable something is (low inherent variability), the easier it is to model. But, then, if its easily predictable, why do you need the model?

Earlier, we observed that physical systems are typically more easily modeled than human systems. That's because they are subject to less variability over time. How they work tends at least to remain within an envelope bounded by the immutable laws of physics.

The laws of human behavior are far more elastic! They rarely change, change slowly over time, or change in an instant, presenting an infinite number of possible changes in behavior over a continuum:

Consider behavior that can last a lifetime: Someone

who always goes to church on Sunday (or temple on Saturday or mosque on Friday).

Or behavior that changes slowly but perceptibly over time: My tennis serve isn't what it used to be, and my game has slowly but noticeably deteriorated between ages twenty-five and sixty.

Or something that changes rapidly over time: Hourly data in the operator log shows the measurements were taken promptly until near the end of the midnight shift when the operator apparently fell asleep on the job.

Something that changes abruptly, but quickly returns to the preceding level: Your heart is said to stop when you sneeze.

Something that changes and can't even be quantified or measured: I feel more energetic after I take a particular nutritional supplement.

Feelings are difficult to measure, and therefore some outcome dependent on feelings is darn near impossible to model. This is far from a trivial problem in a time when social psychologists model emotions like "happiness."

I was hopeful at 8:20 am when my floor installers showed up. I was frustrated at 8:30 am when they told me they'd have to reschedule and it would cost an extra $400. My "happiness" quotient changed dramatically.

Experts can pretty accurately model the performance of my car's engine. That's because the physical characteristics of the engine are likely to change relatively slowly over time. The primary input, gasoline, is a reasonably standardized product with little variation. The other primary input, air, changes mostly with temperature and humidity. The effect of these two variables on performance is well understood and reasonably predictable. Calculations for auto performance are somewhat standardized. There isn't much variation or "change" going on.

Most physical processes are similar. The operation and performance of even a complex facility like a petroleum refinery can be modeled in a way so practical that it can be automated, requiring very few human attendants (or at least far fewer than, say, three decades ago). As long as the variations in the raw material (petroleum) are accounted for in the models, along with other variables which can be pretty accurately measured and whose impact on the process is well documented, all is well.

Built physical systems, even ones with lots of moving parts and dynamic characteristics, are where models shine. When the dynamic characteristics, interactions, and variations get more complex, models are less effective or even completely useless, or they are effective only within narrow ranges of conditions. Atmospheric, biological, environmental, and other natural processes are good examples.

As a quick review, modeling physical systems is difficult, modeling natural processes is really difficult. Accurately modeling human behavior, well, that's almost impossible.

When you begin to model human behavior, especially collective human behavior, modeling gets dicey in a hurry. That is, the model (as a predictor of some objective reality) may not be much better than a random generator. Yet every day, "experts" strive to create models which can tell us things about how happy we are, how hopeful we are, and how much joy we have in our lives. (And how we're going to vote based on all those things.)

If you don't believe me, just do a quick Internet search. I did, and turned up an academic paper in which it is suggested that objective happiness can best be measured by tracking and aggregating people's momentary good and bad feelings. The researchers formulate a theoretical model to capture the unique effects of positive emotions.

I don't mean to disparage the research described in this paper. I do wish to question models constructed to reveal some objective reality about something as difficult to define, measure, and articulate as human emotion. The potential errors are huge.

Your respective definitions of hope, happiness, and joy are different from mine. You can place values on human emotions. Sometimes these values are misconstrued as measurements. At least be aware that they are very different from scientific measurements.

The difference between a value and an actual measurement looms large when we go the next step and learn about the five co-words, what I consider the heart and soul of numerical analysis and modeling.

8. SUSPECT THE CO(MPANY) THEY KEEP

Five words beginning with co- (and, sadly, one that doesn't fit my cute rule) have to be pressed into service whenever you see numbers being used to support a result, a trend, recommendation, decision, action, or conclusion. They are co-location, coincidence, correlation, causation, convergence, and consensus. They also comprise a spectrum ranging from absurdity to the foundation for human knowledge

In numerical analysis, we dwell at the absurdity end of this range all too often.

Co-location—this is when two things are located or occur around the same time or place. You might see two of your friends at a new store in town and conclude all three of you like to experience new stores ahead of the crowd.

I was in Manhattan last summer and noticed that there appeared to be lots of people of one generic ethnic composition everywhere. I concluded that the percentage of these people living in New York was higher than the last time I visited, and certainly higher than when I lived there or commuted there twenty years ago.

When I casually mentioned this to a friend (current Manhattan resident) over coffee, she said, "Yeah, they are the only people who can afford Manhattan anymore." In a brief time, my observation of co-location turned into a stronger association or relationship, not to mention, one with some prejudicial overtones.

A friend from the suburbs in a different state came to visit our new location in a city neighborhood in a new state and observed groups of people hanging around at various places on the street. They continued on through the neighborhood and then stopped to call us because they wondered if they had taken a wrong turn or were in the wrong place, the implication being that people of a particular generic ethnic or racial group hanging around the streets might make our neighborhood unsafe.

If it seems offensive to even bring up such examples, realize that all of us make these erroneous "judgments" all the time, even if we don't want to admit it publicly or even to ourselves. But the truth is that we survive by making instinctive judgments in real time. It's called situational awareness. We need to explain things as they happen, and humans don't like uncertainty. So we construct a model or fit what we see and experience into a pre-constructed, preconceived model of the way the world works. And because of that, it's easy to turn co-location into something more than it deserves.

When I was just entering puberty, I remember a period one summer when I would sit on our front porch (truth be known, I was grounded and had nothing to do) at the same time every day. Soon, I noticed these two girls who lived on the other side of the circle from us walk by our house around the same time.

I considered this co-location—their time to walk was scheduled around the same time as when I planted my butt in that rocking chair. Come to find out, they were deliberately timing their walks to see me, in the hopes that I would be mature enough to chat them up. This nugget of information came from my sister who had talked to them, and who reported that one of the girls had expressed an interest in me. (I was not mature enough, by the way.)

I wish I had been better at such pattern recognition when I was younger.

Coincidence—this is similar to co-location except that the co-location is a random event. It is a coincidence that you attended the same event as some prince or potentate twice in one week; neither your presence nor his was scheduled. It's not an indication that you are among royalty, or that you yourself are royalty.

Much statistical analysis is aimed at ensuring that results of experiments are not coincidental or, for that matter, random. If you flip a coin a thousand times, chances are almost guaranteed that the coin will be heads 500 times and tails 500 times, or pretty damn close.

That's a statistical result. It may be only coincidental that twelve subjects out of twenty in a pharmacological study showed an improvement, or that your hedge fund beat the general stock market's performance for one quarter.

If I observe a high percentage of one ethnic group in the expensive seats at Yankee stadium, I might erroneously believe this supports my earlier (prejudicial) observation that Manhattan is being taken over by said ethnic group. How would I have known that a tour bus of visitors with tickets in that section had arrived before the game?

Correlation—this is when you can show, through observation or statistical analysis, that a change to an input or variable has some association to a change in an output or another variable. Correlations can be weak or strong, depending on statistical analysis.

Correlation is a giant step up from coincidence.

Suppose a superstar ball player is acquired for a losing team. Almost immediately, the team begins to win more games, but the superstar's stats have declined. Is it just a co-location or coincidence and the losing team would have started winning at the same point in the season anyway? Or is there a correlation? Perhaps the superstar brought "desperately needed leadership" (as a sportswriter might say) to the team, an outcome that would be hard to quantify? If five of the eight other starters were interviewed and they claimed that the superstar seemed to have an effect on their quality of play, would that support a correlation?

Correlations get stronger if the effect can be repeated. A sports sociologist might analyze team performance for many teams over many seasons after a superstar is brought on board. The study might show that there is indeed a statistically significant effect between hiring a superstar and team performance, regardless of how well the superstar played. But did one cause the other? And does the better performance last? And could a coach use that information to convince the team's owner to spring $50 million for a superstar's ten year contract?

Such correlations could be ripe for beer slurping banter sitting in the hot sun during a game. It's a deadly serious matter when it comes to, say, showing a beneficial effect of a new drug, or the efficacy of an investment thesis.

Causation (our term without a "co")—this refers to when one thing is responsible for another thing happening. When your finger pushes over the first domino in a line, and it causes the second domino to fall, and it causes the third domino to fall, etc., that's causation. I can be pretty sure that the bruise on my face when I woke up was caused by the guy who slugged me in the bar the night before. However, if I passed out drunk and my head hit the edge of the bar before I went down, maybe not. If the case went to trial, a jury would have to decide.

Causation is a giant leap from correlation, just like correlation is a giant step from coincidence.

Consider the coin toss again. Chances are, over 100 tosses, 50 will turn up heads and 50 tails, according to the laws of probability. There's no cause and effect. It's just a statistical "fact." This is a really important point. Researchers can determine relationships between values and show statistically that they are valid. Statistical validity doesn't mean the result is actually useful in the real world.

I study ten baseball teams who have hired a superstar over fifty seasons, and out of five hundred team-seasons, there are three hundred instances of better team performance. Is that statistically significant? If it was exactly two-hundred fifty, is that just blind chance, or something more? Maybe the better question is how I discern "better" team performance.

The most important question is, did the hiring of the superstar cause the improved team performance? Can you really answer this? Numerical analysis will certainly lead more people to believe you can.

Let's return to MEDTRIP A. At what point can researchers conclude that MEDTRIP A is responsible for improved cognitive ability? Perhaps more importantly, at what point can a patient conclude that the improved cognitive ability is worth the cost of a patented pharmaceutical, beyond the assurance that the insurance company has been convinced to cover it. Or, is the improved cognitive ability more than what could be had with an over-the-counter nutritional supplement?

This last one is exceedingly difficult to answer. That's precisely why numerical modeling and statistical analysis are so powerful when used correctly, and devastating when abused.

We also know that weird things lead to spurious results. For example, just the fact of paying attention to someone's cognitive needs can improve their cognitive ability.

Causation is very difficult to substantiate. It's a very high bar when it comes to conclusions based on numerical analysis and modeling.

All the circumstantial evidence in the world suggests that smoking leads to lung cancer, but I don't think to this day anyone has found a direct chemical pathway from nicotine or tar or any other ingredient in tobacco to cancer cells in lungs. At least I haven't found it, and I've been looking and asking just because I'm curious.

In *Merchants of Doubt*, Naomi Oreskes and Erik Conway explain in detail how tobacco companies funded a "disinformation campaign" to turn the tide away from public and political pressure on smoking. But in the world of doubt, there are at least two kinds, especially when justice is being applied. There is the "beyond a reasonable" variety and the "beyond a shadow of" variety. I'll leave it to readers to decide whether this quote from their book shows causation:

"Current science does not allow us to say with certainty that any one particular person's lung cancer—no matter how much she smoked—was caused by smoking. There are always other possibilities. The science does tell us that a person with a twenty-year, three-pack a day habit who has lung cancer most probably got that cancer from smoking, because other causes of cancer are very rare." (p. 31)

It's still a probabilistic assessment, not a deterministic one. And please don't consider this an excuse to keep smoking or to start. There are many reasons not to smoke that have nothing to do with cancer or heart disease or other health concerns.

Convergence occurs when many people are studying the same thing and their results begin to look similar.

Smoking bans, exposure of children to lead, radiation leakage from nuclear sources, and many other societal ills now governed by complex and expensive regulatory frameworks are derived from the convergence of many studies on similar results.

The statistician who gets the most respect for his election year polling analyzes the results of all the other polls. His is a poll of polls. He looks for convergence among the different approaches. He also has a twist that others don't: He factors in the success of each of these polls in predicting past events, and weights successful polls higher than less successful ones. It's an example of a feedback loop into the model.

When a client asks me to develop a market forecast for a product or service, the first thing I do is review every other forecast I can find and see if there is any convergence. I use this as a benchmark, and then try to develop a more rational forecast methodology. For my clients, the accuracy of the forecast is less important than the logic of developing one. The methodology has to be defensible.

This so-called meta-data approach still is not a substitute for causation. Twenty studies which, from a statistical perspective, irrefutably show a correlation between smoking and lung cancer (and heart disease and other health effects) is an ironclad correlation, but still not cause. A chemical pathway from chemical compounds in tobacco to cancer cells reveals probable cause.

Another danger with convergence is something I run up against when I have to develop a market forecast. Often, I find half a dozen public sources in my review but most of them will have used the same core numbers in their forecast. In other words, each has "adapted" the market research from one other source. Six variations of the same thing may be a convergence of opinion, but not convergence on an objective truth.

Consensus—Finally, whether you have true causation or convergence of indirect, investigative, or circumstantial evidence, you still must achieve consensus. Other experts have validated your methods and your results. Your results are repeatable. Consensus also means that other people (who may not be experts) believe you as well.

Studies have shown that up to 70 percent of academic research is not repeatable. Such research is merely an academic exercise, until it is repeatable.

Consensus is critical. Over the years, I have had many doubts about global warming forecasts with respect to measurement error; numerical modeling of complex, non-linear, and dynamic atmospheric processes; and the associated political motivations and biases.

However, I cannot ignore that the vast majority of scientists in the climate field, as well as scientists of all stripes, have achieved a high level of consensus on the matter, perhaps not on the forecasted absolute rate of temperature rise but certainly on the perilous direction we're headed.

Consensus among specialists does not mean consensus among the population at large. The person elected president of the United States in 2016 stated during the campaign that climate change was a hoax perpetrated by the Chinese. Consensus for national and international response to climate change has to be achieved with tens of millions of people.

Often, though, consensus only has to be reached among a few people. The maker of MEDTRIP A only needs the consensus of the few specialists familiar with drug testing protocols, the regulators at the Food and Drug Administration (FDA) reviewing the tests and making judgments for drug release dates and regulatory frameworks, a few "early adopter" MDs, and insurance firms willing to reimburse patients.

Professional consensus is different from general consensus of the electorate. The forecasts I develop in my consulting practice usually require consensus between myself and my client. Often, I will ask a few colleagues to backstop and review my methodology. That is sufficient for the client's need for an independent expert opinion.

How many economists' models were forecasting an average of 2 percent inflation for the next thirty years after the "misery index" (inflation rate + prime interest rate) years of the late 1970s/early 1980s, when inflation was often between 5-10 percent? Today, how many are willing to bet that high inflation will be a serious threat in the future after two decades of tame inflation?

It sounds tautological (defined simply as a useless restatement), but models are best at predicting things that are easily predictable. Many times, they are used to confirm things that are obvious. At the same time, note that the few economists credited with forecasting the global financial crash of 2007-2008 are the dark cloud types—they forecast catastrophe all the time! I used to tell my kids—live long enough in the forecasting business and you'll eventually be right. A few economists are 24/7/365 contrarians always forecasting gloom and doom, so they're bound to be right at some point.

Always view with suspicion the (co)mpany kept by any number, value, result, trend, or numerical conclusion. Experts do research. Many of our so-called experts research one thing, and they need to keep showing progress in order to keep being paid. Showing a correlation earlier rather than later helps their cause.

Media companies have lots of pages and screens and time slots to fill "informing" their audiences. Most journalists, writers, bloggers, and talking heads have no clue about distinguishing between correlation, causation, and consensus. They only "report" what experts, elected officials, and other sources tell them. The only standards for reporting are first, having at least two sources, and second, reporting both sides (or all sides) fairly. How many media outlets today adhere to these standards?

Many different people need to arrive at a result from different directions for it to be valid. Each result has to scale higher and higher bars for validity, truth, and "objective reality." Then people who often don't have the means to understand what the experts tell them also have to be persuaded.

The road from coincidence to consensus is a long and winding one. That's why people often look for other ways to show the significance of their work. One of the best is to lean on credentials, the subject of the next commandment.

9. HOLD CREDENTIALS AT ARMS LENGTH

We live in a rock star, celebrity-driven world. There's no getting around this. It's a condition of our current society. What's more, we live in free-agent nation, a society in which individuals have to maintain control of their employment destiny.

In short, everyone is looking out for number one. There are fewer institutions—government, unions, corporations, and institutions offering long-term stable employment or support—to provide economic stability. We're all looking for a competitive edge, to extend our earning potential, whether it's consulting from one's academic platform, becoming a go-to expert for the media in your area of expertise, leveraging your expertise into media celebrity, managing your own "brand," telling your story through self-publishing, seeking funding for a venture startup around your patent, or propagating your artistry (music, arts) through on-line and social media tools and techniques.

In this arena, those who know how to apply (or can pay for) sophisticated numerical analysis can run roughshod over those who can't.

Many journalism majors who go on to become reporters, editors, talking heads, and media gate keepers don't learn much math along the way. Lawyers and politicians typically don't get rigorous training in applied math and sciences; they hire "expert witnesses" (consultants like me). Banks are not typically managed by people who intimately understand sophisticated econometric models. Their executives instead come through the ranks in trading, sales, customer service, and government relations, deal-makers and negotiators in other words.

This is why Wall Street depletes the ranks of graduating physicists. In the past these scientists may have gone to NASA or into basic research in academia, but today, they're more likely to work behind the scenes building and running the quant models bankers use as a competitive edge. Current reports in the media are that experts with these same "quant" capabilities are now rushing to Silicon Valley to analyze big data and automate all things digital.

The gatekeepers of modern society, in other words, those in power, are not generally people who understand math models or how they are applied. When presented with decisions involving numerical analysis, therefore, they tend to rely on people they already know and trust.

I got my first taste of the attitudes of venture capitalists early in my career. My brother had been awarded a patent for an invention. He formed a true "garage" company around his invention. He got his family members involved early on (he learned that lesson and never did that again). I lined him up with a guy I knew well who could help the fledgling company raise venture capital.

After my friend's initial meetings with VCs where he presented my brother's company, he told me privately, "I can raise money on the strength of your brother but not his partner." I asked why. He responded, candidly, "Your brother has a doctorate degree from Cal Berkeley and an undergraduate degree from Cornell [Ivy League]; his partner has a BA from University of Alabama."

Reputation sells!

Such sentiments have been validated over and over again in my forty-year career. One of my businesses later in my career was helping clean energy tech clients raise venture capital. VCs can hire all the experts they want to help them understand a company, its market, and its technology. But when the last power point slide has been shown, and it's time for the go/no-go decision and write a check, many of them rely, not on actual knowledge of the technology, but what I call the comfort envelope— where degrees are from, how the company presents itself, whether the CEO has a track record of raising money for a previous company, how many people they know in common, and who they pal around with at the monthly meeting of the local investors group.

Credentials play an outsized role in the decision, even if it's the meteorologist on the nightly news.

This is true with academics, corporate researchers, and authors who popularize science and technical concepts for the masses. A doctor with celebrity status becomes less of a "subject matter expert." He's an expert at being interviewed, at translating "knowledge" into sound bites, at manipulating an audience, creating a narrative, and telling a story. He may have been an acclaimed expert at one time. After a time, the expert becomes a brand and brand protection becomes the objective.

Just because a financial modeling expert works at a premier Wall Street firm doesn't mean her econometric model is any better than a lady in the back office of the Triple X Fund. But I can almost guarantee you the top five Wall Street bank gal will be quoted more often and get more high-level meetings with potential investors. Her credentials, her "brand equity," is far higher.

A climate model constructed and used at MIT may not be the best in the world, or even one of the best, but we can probably agree that an institution like MIT will be the recipient of more grant money to study climate behavior because, well, it's MIT.

Clever authors working for renowned media channels

or universities come up with slogans like "tipping point" and "flat world" and build theories about collective behavior around them. For a while, the "model" (or metaphor) works. Writers at *Small Town News Gazette* usually don't get the same book publishing offers as the ones who write for national branded publications even if their models or metaphors are just as "valid" or just as powerful.

Many of the mathematical models used as the foundation of modern life have little to do with rigorous mathematics or expert modeling capabilities, and more to do with the credentials of the modelers. Highly regarded experts spawn like-minded colleagues simply because they were in the same department at university or worked with the expert at the same company or government agency.

Unfortunately, bias propagates through tightly interconnected webs of credentialed experts the same way error and uncertainty propagate through equations. That's because of something none of us can do much about: the human condition.

10. RESPECT THE HUMAN CONDITION

The story behind every reported number or numerical result is also the story of the human condition. The work "painted" through a numbers-based narrative exhibits all the flaws and wonders of the human beings who conceived the story.

Darwinists would likely say that consensus has been reached on the strength of natural selection as "objective reality." Global warming alarmists are convinced that planetary warming and greater extremes in climate are inexorable unless nations and people change how they live.

But even once consensus is reached, belief has to follow for anything to change. Leaders aren't leaders without followers. So what to make of the large fraction of the American population who identify as evangelicals, who discount natural selection, and whose faith continues to be derived from biblical teachings? Who is to say that Darwinists can't practice their own version of faith in a scientific principle? How we view religion vs. science, surely an enduring facet of the human condition if there ever was one, will affect whether we are part of the "consensus" on such matters.

What is belief? Is consensus when ninety percent of experts in a field say something is occurring and fifty-six percent of the general population (as may be revealed in opinion polls) concurs? This is actually the state of "belief" in global climate change as a problem requiring immediate changes to collective behavior to rectify, according to one poll I just looked at. Ten years ago, both of those percentages were lower.

People who analyze the same FBI crime statistics arrive at contradictory conclusions. Looked at one way, they might lead some citizens to live in gated communities and arm themselves with guns. Looked at another way, they can show inherent bias towards crime and criminals in ethnic communities. Predispositions towards fear, the communities of "others," and personal safety, all aspects of the human condition, influence how we view such statistics.

While writing this chapter, I was struck by two things I heard on television during this polarized election season. One was an "expert" on Iran describing the veneer of democracy in that country. He noted that the leaders who run for president have to be selected and blessed by a large council of bureaucrats. The "tone" of this expert suggested (to me) that Iran was no democracy at all.

Not one hour later, I listened to a media pundit interview the head of the Democratic National Committee, who explained the role of "super-delegates" in the Democratic Party primary. Ostensibly, super-delegates were instituted by the Party in 1984 to ensure that all the diverse voices of the party are heard in the nomination process. But super-delegates, by other accounts, are there to prevent the nomination of a probable loser in the general election.

In terms of data science, super-delegates help prevent the nomination of someone who is too much of an "outlier" in the political and cultural spectrum. Super-delegates enrich the "fudge" in the democratic primary process.

In fact, the Democratic National Committee (DNC) and the Republican National Committee (RNC) are large collections of "operatives" and loyalists whose function is to guide and manipulate the election process "behind the scenes" to ensure that the party wins elections. In earlier times, this was called the "smoked-filled rooms."

The strength of the two parties is the reason no independent party candidate has won a presidential election in modern times. One of the primary tools of each party is how they are able to manipulate the numbers.

Super-delegates are fifteen percent of those who nominate the Democratic candidate at the convention. But each state awards delegates to winners of the primaries in ways that don't necessarily reflect the percentage of the popular vote. And each state primary, especially the "big ones," are designed to make sure the party has as much influence as possible without being too obvious about it.

This gets back to my core objection with numerical analysis. It's the transparency of modeling and numerical analysis which has to improve, not that modeling and painting stories with numbers are wrong.

In fact, the numerical aspects of electioneering began with the framers of our Constitution and continue to this day through "gerrymandering"—the process by which both parties alter the perimeters of voting districts based on population statistics to favor the election of their party's candidate. The original Electoral College of the Framers is the reason why, two and a half centuries later, six states hold enormous sway over the outcome of every presidential election (New York, California, Florida, Texas, Ohio, and Illinois).

Simply, if you win these six states, you are awarded enough of the electoral math to win. They are the most populous states.

Our democracy isn't a people's democracy (and wasn't meant to be); it's a republic that relies on elected representatives as proxies to do the people's bidding. That's what the Framers wanted. They also wanted a federal government that would never be able to centralize too much power over the states. That's why so many court battles boil down to states rights vs. federal authority, why every piece of federal legislation is implemented through a state implementation program, and why every legislative move can be challenged in the courts by anyone with the money and will to do so.

So, while during the primary season, pundits talked about super delegates, since the election, the talk has turned to the role of the Electoral College, our "council" of men and women picked at the state level who actually vote for the President of the United States with little or no regard for who won the popular vote.

Is America the same as Iran when it comes to democracy? No. Do both countries have institutional mechanisms, backed by complex numbers games, to ensure that those in power remain in power, and outsiders have as little chance of taking over the reins of government as possible? Yes.

How you view the analysis of two "democracies" I just constructed depends on the extent to which you "feel" national pride, your desire for national security, your inputs from the media about geopolitical issues, and many other factors.

How you feel vs. how you think are fundamental aspects of the human condition. One may be rational and the other may be irrational, but one is no less real to you than the other.

Earlier I mentioned a relatively new pharmaceutical for patients with Alzheimer's and how I recently accompanied my father on a visit to his neurologist, who prescribed this new drug. I'm not a physician, but even a cursory review of the public information on the drug, especially what was available on the pharma company's own website, made me suspect that this drug was not ready for prime time, at least not for my father. There were too many squishy words in the narrative painted by the company.

The most important statement was that the drug does nothing to reverse the process of Alzheimer's but may slow some of the symptoms for up to 6-12 months. Yet the doctor had said that in clinical trials the large population who took the drug had experienced beneficial effects compared to a control group. I wondered how he defined "beneficial effects."

My dad has Cadillac health insurance. He would pay next to nothing to add this drug to his health maintenance regimen. The human condition in a consumer-oriented society like ours suggests I should let my father try it and see. It's basically free, right? It should "do no harm."

But when I apply my commandments, the numerical support for taking this drug doesn't add up. Above all else, how does a 92-year old man in the early to middle stages of Alzheimer's even articulate how much better his short-term memory is? Correspondingly, how would I, the dutiful son, quantify the benefit, not for a group of subjects in a clinical trial, but for one individual, my father? A father who, as a PhD chemical engineer, spent his entire adult life emphasizing the importance of evaluating critical decisions through the lens of applied quantitative analysis. If he could, he would analyze and quantify the benefits himself, so his children should do no less.

The doctor isn't necessarily prescribing this new drug based on the specific neurological capabilities of my father, but on the strength of aggregate testing with statistical validation of at least a modicum of benefit. That wasn't good enough for me.

A recent *New York Times* article reports that "there are so many different hospital ratings that more than 1,600 medical centers can now lay claim to being included on a 'top 100' honor roll, grade A, or "best" hospitals list. The ratings, all based on metrics of outcomes and processes, have become important because hospitals compete, not so much for the attention of the patient, but for the dollars of the insurance companies and the grant money of the National Institutes of Health.

Part of the human condition is to compete for limited resources.

The problem with these ratings is that the hospitals are not using a standardized methodology that would allow the consumer to adequately make a comparison. Rather, these ratings are "one-offs," designed for marketing purposes. The use of the rating system isn't egregious, the lack of explanation about the limitations and purpose is.

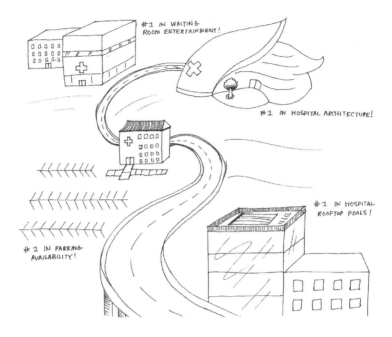

While my wife had her gall bladder removed (at a very highly rated hospital) a few years ago, I sat in the waiting room and was called to the desk every few minutes by the infuriating sound of a buzzer I had to keep with me (like the ones you use to roam around a mall while you wait for a table at a restaurant). This was so I could be told what was happening while she was upstairs. I presumed this was a "best practice" in health care customer service, and had little doubt it was factored into their "rating."

Ostensibly, the spouse, or advocate, was being "kept in the loop."

Ironically, after all that attention to me, the hospital messed up at the back end in post-operative care by writing an incorrect prescription (which made my wife nauseous), discharging her too early (part of cost management—turn over those beds!), and giving us poor instructions on what to do if she was later in pain (we ended up in the emergency room at midnight and we could have just gone straight to the department in charge).

But they sure were great at keeping me informed of her progress, all while I was trying to get some work done in the waiting room. I impolitely declined to take the survey they asked me to fill in about my experience.

You might think that accounting—basic addition and subtraction—is as straight up as a numerical-based profession can be, free of biases and flaws in the human condition.

Think again.

Accounting is math, true. Accounting is also governed by standards and guidelines called Generally Accepted Accounting Practices (GAAP). Accounting practices are constantly tweaked by regulatory fiat and standards committees. You can liken it to comparing home run stats over decades as steroids use grows, owners bring in outfield walls, lower pitching mounds, and other actions to make the game more exciting.

Making the rules which govern numerical analysis is part of the collective human condition. Stretching them is, too.

Enron and other energy companies got fat, corrupt, and stupid by abusing an accounting practice called "mark to market." I won't bore you with the details, but essentially the practice (still in effect today) allows a company's financial engineers to value the company's operations by "marking" the near-term value of goods and services in the present at some future market price.

Can you imagine anything as ambiguous as valuing a commodity years into the future based on its price today? Commodities prices vary like crazy. Imagine a couple of bunkers of gasoline in storage valued at today's price at the pump. In my area, that price is as low as $2.00/gal, but five years ago, it was approaching $5/gal. That would inflate the mark to market value by 150 percent.

Still, this wouldn't be such a problem if there were a mark-to-market standard methodology for assigning future value which all companies followed. Having a standard or reference value (remember the atomic clock) helps minimize sources of bias and error.

The corruption in Enron's case and the energy industry at large was allowing every company to use their own methodology. At the time, Enron just happened to paint the best story out of those numbers for Wall Street analysts. Predictably, Enron fell the hardest when the day of reckoning arrived. Other companies were punished severely. Many Enron look-alikes folded. And Enron's accounting firm folded as well.

Another aspect of the human condition is to "follow

the herd" when the herd is achieving something you want to achieve. Bad things happen when the herd practices numerical modeling and analysis that is fundamentally flawed, unfairly structured with preferences and biases, or just plain corrupt.

Speaking of the herd, here's a chilling example. Richard Nisbett, the author of *Mindware: Tools for Smart Thinking* (described in Appendix 1) and a professor of psychology at the University of Michigan has launched a crusade against multiple regression analysis (MRA), the most popular statistical analysis technique used in the social sciences (and science and engineering in general). He goes as far to advocate that articles in the media should come with a warning similar to that for smoking: "Caution—these data are based on MRA."

I'll describe the problem he cites with this anecdote. You can pull a great sound bite for a movie out of an awful review. "The film was wildly comical for the first fifteen minutes; then it fell flat." You might read on the film producer's newspaper advertisement, "Wildly comical…"

Similarly, MRA allows the analyst to take one variable out from the host of variables which might affect an outcome and draw a correlation. It's like isolating a relationship between two variables, developing a numerical value for it, and ignoring all the other interrelationships with other variables.

The reality of the herd mentality is that people tend to gravitate towards techniques which appear to work, or are successful. Investors pile into a stock when it's flying high. We go to movies that win awards. Academics, probably unknowingly, abuse MRA because it serves purposes other than depicting the objective reality they seek.

Just to keep your head spinning, the herd mentality leads to something called "framework error," or the assumptions made by an accepted means of analyzing uncertainty. While the consensus may be that MRA is suitable and adequate for most research analysis, according to Nisbett, that doesn't mean it's the most robust approach.

The first technical presentation I made at an industry meeting (knees-knocking, generally ill-prepared) was co-authored with a statistician who revealed to me for the first time that the standard "bell curve" wasn't the only way to apply statistics to a data set (in our case, size measurements of flyash particles sampled in a power plant flue gas duct). We used something called the Weibull distribution.

Our data showed two "humps," or the possible presence of two averages rather than one. A Weibull distribution "fit" our bimodal data better. Part of the human condition is to explain why something happened. We crave certainty. We want answers. In this case, a Weibull distribution explained what our data was trying to reveal better than a standard distribution. At the time, I wondered how many other possible "distributions" are there?

Just like every number has to carry the burden of its errors, every numerical answer derived is a product of a model, and models are constructed with all the vagaries of the human condition. Perhaps the most important of those vagaries is the temptation to start with the answer and work backward, which is the subject of our next chapter.

11. DON'T START WITH THE ANSWER

This is a hard precept to adhere to when it comes to numerical modeling. As explained earlier, models are constructed to test and ultimately validate a theory or hypothesis by fitting data from observed or experimental conditions. The hope is that the model can be used to extrapolate or infer reasonably valid information and conclusions from new data for new situations.

Most quant exercises these days, unfortunately, seem to begin with the answer and work backwards. Some of this affliction stems from the business model discussed earlier. Often, the "answer" sought will be derived from:

- An ideology—"Free markets are better than government programs!" Or vice versa.
- Ego—I'm right. I know it. I just need more evidence.
- Institutional bias—An organization responsible for regulating an industry will generally err on the side of more regulation. An organization with a fiduciary duty to its stockholders will

generally err on the side of boosting the stock price.

- Hierarchical behavior—What the boss wants, the boss gets.

Thus, the objective of too much modeling today is to manufacture reality, rather than reveal insights about objective reality. Start with the answer, the reality you want, then work backwards.

Pharmaceutical companies follow testing protocols and numerical analyses which are accepted by government regulators and approved by industry standards committees. This is part of the objective reality framework.

Another reality, though, is such companies wish to accelerate growth in product sales. It is, in fact, their fiduciary duty to increase shareholder value (if they are a public company), maximize the value of the eventual exit (if a venture-backed company), or otherwise achieve the goals of the business. This applies to non-profits as well.

The consultant who evaluates the cost/benefit of adding a new kind of asset to the electricity grid is assisting his client to penetrate an old-line conservative industry with new technology. All of his work is probably going to tend towards an answer that shows the greatest benefit possible. (For the same reasons I've written this book, I am not that kind of consultant.)

Global climate denial folks continue to refine and tweak their models to show why climate change is not the threat the other side says it is. Both sides, in fact, are using their own models to create a reality called fear—in the one case fear about catastrophic impact on future generations from business as usual and in the other case fear about the deleterious effect of strict policy on economic growth and personal well-being and liberty. The difference is there is vastly larger consensus that the threat is real and urgent, and not benign.

In too many cases, researchers start with a position derived from an ideological framework or with a need to satisfy a client's competitive position and work backward. These are answers, not assessments. The modelers are advocates, not independent sources, scientists, or sober academics.

Social media companies use algorithms to match advertisements to preferences derived from aggregated usage data from their sites. It's no wonder that companies trying to sell me double A batteries show up in my feed when I've just done a search on energy storage (it's not even close to the right kind of storage, but it has some of the same search words).

In my college-bound youth, I caught myself biasing my college ratings on those key parameters I mentioned in the introduction. I had in mind a college I preferred. I wasn't interested in a numerical result which provided objective insight into my decision. I was trying to appease my father while making sure I didn't blow my chance at attending the college of my choice. The boss is always right, right? The guy who is funding the work (or paying the tuition) has to be appeased.

I read reports from Washington DC think tanks, alias the beltway bandits, all the time, especially in the energy, economics, and environmental areas. It's no wonder that "progressive" leaning think tanks use consultants and advisors to conduct studies which, strangely, never seem to come up with conclusions that would support a conservative political position, and vice versa. In the case of labor issues, what progressive think tank is going to produce a white paper with lots of numbers and graphs which doesn't support a raise in the minimum wage? Conservative think tanks operate the same way, of course.

Maybe the better way to state this rule is, thou shalt not start with advocacy and work backwards.

One of my favorite magazines as a teenager was *Mad*. I've often thought a book I should write before I die is "Everything I know I Learned from *Mad Magazine*." I still remember this one two-frame drawing. In the first frame an old guy stands on a soapbox with a sign that reads, "Money is the root of all evil," and in the second frame a guy stands next to him with a sign next to his sign that adds, "The lack of ..."

When you assess numbers rationally without fear or favor, you sometimes wonder whether anyone is making any progress towards "objective reality." Global climate change is permanently altering the inhabitability of our planet. Or, global climate change has been occurring for millennia and there's really nothing mankind needs to do about it. Both of these broad conclusions are backed up to the hilt with numerical analysis by seasoned and rational scientists—though as I stated earlier, the vast majority agree with the former conclusion over the latter.

If the phrase once was "Money talks, BS walks," today the phrase should be "BS swaggers if money buys numerical evidence." The data doesn't lie, or so the quants love to say. Managers love to say, we make only evidence-based decisions!

Perhaps nowhere have models been applied with the answer in mind as keenly as in financial engineering. Suppose you are a representative of a Wall Street firm. You have an exotic new investment product you wish to sell. It's not easy to sell something that has never been sold before. One of the tools you bring to bear on the problem of "making a market" for your product is to create a model that will assign a value to this new investment vehicle. Accuracy of the model isn't as important as the client's faith in the credibility of the modeler.

Credibility often has little to do with error and accuracy, or objective reality. It has everything to do with what someone is willing to believe (human condition), and who is telling them the story (credentials).

Donald MacKenzie, a Scottish sociologist, conducted an impressive amount of research to support a theory that one of the most famous financial models of all time, the Black Scholes model for calculating the value of a financial derivative, drove the market in derivatives and commodities futures. The model created the reality of a derivatives market because, with the Black Scholes equation, there was a means of calculating the value of trading a contract into the future. Ends justify the means. Start with the answer.

As long as experts in the investment community can agree on a method for valuation of an investment, a market can be created to trade them.

This type of modeling is common to Wall Street firms. The models are designed to inflate the value of something and extract a commensurately higher fee transacting that something. Models like Black Scholes gave derivative contracts financial legitimacy. They make them credible to investors with lots of money to put at risk.

If you need proof, MacKenzie's book (described further in Appendix 1), *An Engine, Not a Camera* (an engine drives something, a camera takes an image to represent something in reality), notes that in 1970, the volume of trading in financial derivatives such as futures was very small. Models like Black Scholes, which began to be created and applied around the same time, supported an "authoritative theory of finance." By 2004, the market for derivatives contracts was in the trillions of dollars, hundreds of trillions if you add them one way, tens of trillions if you add them up another way. Regardless, it's a huge, huge number.

Several other excellent books are available on how models are used to create reality, make markets, and inflate the value of the products and contracts the "Street" peddles to investors.

But this isn't just the 1 percent playing with their money. As the world discovered during the 2007-2008 global financial crisis, the 2001 tech and dot com crash, the Savings & Loan scandal of the late 1980s, and other financial market meltdowns, these contracts, and the models which support them, prop up the stock market, home mortgages, corporate bonds, US Treasury Bills, savings accounts, and every other economic and investment vehicle of "modern society." When everything goes up in flames, the 99 percent gets burned the most.

Starting with the answer and working backward is what many of the financial, cultural, and political elite do. And most error occurs when they apply modeling techniques developed for physical systems to human systems. As we will discover in the next chapter, physical systems and human systems have few similarities when it comes to modeling.

12. DON'T CONFUSE HUMAN SYSTEMS WITH PHYSICAL SYSTEMS

One of the greatest threats to the integrity of modeling and numerical analysis is applying analytical techniques meant for certain systems or situations to situations the technique was never meant for.

Statistical and numerical analysis can be applied to any data set. That's why it is so popular. Height and weight measurements, clicks on a website or social media page, ocean temperature measurements at four hundred locations, blood pressure, heart rate … these are parameters which lend themselves to accurate measurements which can then be analyzed or used as inputs in models and equations.

Carbon dating is a technique that has been proven through convergence and scientific consensus to provide highly accurate indirect measurement of age in geologic time scales (since most geologic formations don't come with a circa three million B.C. stamp on them). It is an example of a protocol, a method, an analytical tool, which is applied with extraordinary confidence.

Suppose I participate in an experiment about pain at the dentist's office. I'm told to express the pain I am feeling during ultrasonic cleaning on a scale from 1-10. My sensitivity to pain is going to be much different from someone else's. We could make the reading more "accurate" by having me push a button every time I feel pain and not release the button until the pain goes away. These readings could then be converted into numerical data describing how I feel pain.

But are they any more accurate? As just one complicating factor, if I am constantly subjected to pain, wouldn't my baseline level change, and a "new normal" appear? How might my response to pain change if a lovely hygienist is administering the test and I subconsciously don't wish to appear "weak" in front of her?

Pain is a human feeling difficult to quantify across many individuals. The human body is a physical system, but the level of pain felt has a physical transmission component (from the site of the pain to the brain) as well as an emotional component. The more vague the parameter, the harder it is to "measure" anything of significance.

Even with direct measurements, looking for very tiny changes can involve large sources of error. In other words, it's easier to measure the difference in the temperature of a glass of tap water after it is taken from the faucet and then again after ice is dumped into it. The differential will be large. That's less true if you measure the temperature of a glass of water before and after it is left on the counter for thirty minutes. The differential is much smaller.

An ocean is a HUGE thermal sink, as we engineers might say. Insight into global climate change might require that we monitor differences of a small fraction of a degree centigrade or Fahrenheit between today and hundreds of years ago. The inaccuracies in such measurements are potentially significant.

Generally, the smaller the variation we are trying to capture, the more error will be associated with the measurement.

Large effectively open systems like the ocean with tides and currents and varying depths, etc. are difficult enough to model, especially compared to the behavior of water in a bathtub, a pond, or even a lake. Human behavior is even more difficult to model. And yet, every day, every hour, we are bombarded with news reports and media accounts which require us to consider the results and consequences of human systems modeled as if they are physical systems with routine measurement points.

With physical systems, you can attach sensors which monitor temperature, pressure, flow, strain, stress, chemical composition, and other variables. Biological systems also lend themselves to monitoring (although each human being is a distinct biological entity). You amass reams of data, and validate developed theories of physical system behavior. Data science modeling supports first principles theories with physical systems, and vice versa.

Individual and collective human behavior requires valid measurements about emotions and responses to stimuli. Every action or behavior is the result of an inordinately complex and dynamic system. When we apply numerical analysis to human systems, we have to be extra careful about the limitations in the modeling, in the measurements, and in the conclusions. The bottom line is: laws for modeling and analyzing physical systems do not translate well into guidelines for modeling and analyzing human behavior.

SECTION II

PUTTING YOUR BS
DETECTOR TO WORK

13. APPLYING THE COMMANDMENTS

With the commandments in hand, it's time to look at examples of experts painting by numbers and try to detect some real world BS. As a caution, I've chosen to analyze a number of newspaper articles and the sources behind them, scholarly papers, essays I've received through social media, and even a technical paper given to me by an industry colleague. In keeping with the spirit of my thesis, I acknowledge the potential for self-selection bias inherent in my choices.

I've chosen sources I came across in my daily life over the months I worked on this book. I wanted the examples to come naturally as I proceed through life every day. I didn't consciously select articles I thought were egregious in their violations. Rather, I tried to select examples from a variety of sources in which numerical analysis is the essential part of the news or information being conveyed. In other words, my intention was not to "stack the deck" in favor of sources which clearly illustrate my points. In most cases, I chose examples without having the least clue where my assessment would take me. Clearly, though, they have been chosen because they illustrate how to apply the commandments outlined in the previous section.

In keeping with the style of this book, I also chose not to include the original sources in the narrative (they are, however, listed in Appendix 2). I'm not trying to incriminate anyone, make a source look ridiculous, or suggest that anyone does not have the right to research or publish whatever subjects they deem fit. My intention in this section is to illustrate, through fun and engaging and diverse examples, how the commandments help us think critically about the numbers bombarding us every hour, every day. As you begin to practice applying the Twelve Commandments, you will come across a multitude of examples, and I would be interested in hearing about any you find particularly compelling.

14. THE DAILY GRIND
(OR GRINDING UP THE USELESS
INFORMATION SHOVED AT US DAILY)

It's a random day in America. I'm reading the daily newspaper from a medium-size city in the South.

The front page (above the fold) includes the headline, "A Boardroom of One's Own: [City] ranked one of the best cities for women-owned businesses."

Between two photos is a table showing the top five cities for women-owned businesses. The city cited in the paper is ranked No. 2. The source of the table is an on-line credit history and financial services site. Many precious column inches are devoted to this story.

When the story continues on page 5 of the front section, another table appears which notes that this city ranked 93rd among the top 150 metro areas for the share of women-owned businesses. It turns out that the "best" on page 1 is never defined, and the website's rankings are referred to once in the article with no additional detail.

The article further notes, directly after the reference to the ranking's source, that the Small Business Administration ranked this city "tops in the support of female owned businesses." Much of the rest of the article, curiously, would lead you to believe that this city is at best fair to middling for women-owned businesses.

The painting by numbers here is so flagrant I can hardly even apply the commandments. There is no methodology for the rankings, no assumptions are identified, no data, no nothing. The headline with "best," in my reading, contradicts the rest of the article.

The most useful commandment here is number 5, question the picture. Someone pulled some numbers out of her you-know-what, created a picture, put it on the front page above the fold, and then described the picture, wasting many column inches.

Newspapers, especially those not considered "newspapers of record," are full of "puff" pieces, most of which should dare readers to wake up and discover how they are being constantly deceived, numerically speaking. This article challenges the definition of "puff."

And speaking of puff, here's another headline from

the same edition of the same newspaper, this one filed under Expert Advice: "Nicotine has a role in quitting cigarettes." It cites a study of 800 smokers who smoked at least five cigarettes a day and "had no desire to quit." These smokers were asked to puff on their regular brand of cigarettes with typical nicotine levels, and cigarettes with varying levels of nicotine, over a period of six weeks. The objective was to see if lower nicotine levels helped them quit, or caused them to smoke more to compensate.

The results were "unexpected." Subjects given the lower nicotine cigarettes smoked 23 percent to 30 percent fewer cigarettes per day than those who smoked cigarettes with typical nicotine levels. The low nicotine smokers had reduced dependence on nicotine and had fewer cravings when they weren't smoking.

How did the researchers find 800 smokers who had no desire to quit? How do you measure that? Just by asking them, "Do you or don't you want to quit smoking?" How did they monitor cravings? What does the 23 to 30 percent refer to? I mean, 23-30 percent less for someone who smokes five cigarettes a day amounts to one or two cigarettes. Someone who smokes two packs a day, or forty cigarettes, 23-30 percent less means more than half a pack.

Perhaps most egregiously, the article does not cite the source for the study. Obviously, there is no way to determine how valid the results are, no way to determine correlation or causation. I detect a fundamental flaw in the assumptions, however. The "desire to quit" seems to be the crux of the study. That's the only way you could conclude that the fewer cigarettes burned by the group can be associated with the lower levels of nicotine, and not some other factor.

Without even finding the source of the study, you can discount this one on the basis of commandment 1, no acknowledgment of error, and commandment 2, no visibility on assumptions.

Applying commandment 6, understand the business model, is also important. Newspapers have to fill those column inches around the ads with something. This applies to the paper of record, too, as we'll see next.

15. BENDING GENDER BIAS

"Male sellers on [Internet auction site] have an edge over women, study says." This is from a national newspaper "of record." The researchers analyzed 630,000 auction transactions in the US on an auction site, and reported that "on average, when men and women with equal selling reputations sold the same products, women received lower prices than men." Later, the article says the study "controlled for seller reputation, experience, number of photos, use of bold lettering, and other elements."

First, I wondered how you control for number of photos AND reputation and experience, but on this site, reputation and experience are boiled down to a numerical value. Which begs the question: How does the site measure seller reputation and experience? By surveying buyers? How many users rate reputation? Does the site ensure that users rating reputation are reputable themselves and not simply out to boost the reputation of a friend or sabotage the reputation of a competitor? One interesting data point from the study is that women were less than 25 percent of the sellers in the auction.

My daughter pointed out that this site uses a five point scale for buyers to rate sellers after a transaction has been completed, and that it is reported down to two decimal places. Most sellers have an average rating of between 4.91 and 4.99, she told me. I'm glad she clarified that. First of all, reporting an average figure to two decimals when the choices are one digit is confusing and suspect. Second, when most sellers have an average rating within a 0.08 spread, it suggests that the differences in buyer ratings may not be significant in the first place.

The account further states that on average, women received 0.88 fewer bids for the same items, 97 cents for every dollar a male got for used items, and 80 cents for every dollar on new items auctioned. What is the significance of these numbers? There are no error bounds around them, even though they are the crux of the conclusion.

Like 0.08 spread in ratings, the significance of a 3 cent difference for used items seems pretty low. This is the kind of number for which an error analysis is critical. Maybe our conclusion is that women do a better job of describing used items than new ones.

The article notes that researchers analyzed the descriptive text sellers used and found that women used "slightly more positive language." How was this measured? Whenever I see the word "slightly," I think the error bounds would probably suggest that it could just as well have been slightly negative, too. Wording differences, the article further notes, did not account for the price gap. No evidence is given for this conclusion.

It's dangerous to make broad conclusions from small variations which may not be significant.

Another interesting aspect of this study: The site does not require a seller to list gender though many sellers self-identify. Everyone knows that on-line avatars do not necessarily describe the person in real life. Could it be that less than a quarter of the sellers are identified as female because many of the others prefer to sell under "male?"

Another inference from the study is that male and female buyers "appeared to treat women sellers the same." How did they come up with this?

Acknowledging error (commandment 1) is critical when conclusions are being drawn from results with very small variation. I am troubled by the blanket assumption (commandment 2), "…when men and women with equal selling reputations sold the same product." I'll bet there's some real squishiness in there, especially since the report also notes that "women tended to have better reputations as sellers, although they tended to have less selling experience."

Maybe the conclusion should have been that women get lower prices in auctions because they have less experience? Or that men and women have a natural tendency to be more complimentary towards women?

Probably the best one can conclude from this study is a confirmation of the obvious: We have inherent, though sub-conscious, gender biases when we shop, and probably when we do most anything. This study suggests that men and women discriminate against women sellers, even on this on-line site, which strives for a neutral buying platform.

The gravest error this article made, however, isn't revealed until the very end. "An earlier version of this article misstated the name of the journal that published the study." The journal first cited is one of the oldest and most highly regarded in its field. The correct source has a recognition factor several orders of magnitude lower.

Commandment 9, credentials matter, makes me wonder how many more readers considered this article seriously the first time around.

The obscure studies and articles, supported by numerical BS, which find their way into our lives are relatively harmless compared to the numbers which have real consequences for the whole world, as the next example shows.

16. VOTE EARLY AND OFTEN

Presidential election years are particularly juicy times to analyze painters and their numbers!

I just read an article entitled, "Clinton, Sanders, and Southern Voters." It makes the point that black voters make up a "disproportionately large share of all Democratic primary voters" in many southern states. Then the article notes, "black voters are not monolithic and of one mind," and that there are a hundred ways to analyze the factions within the black community. As if to immediately contradict this, one sentence later, we find: "There isn't one black America, but two, the children of the Great Migration and the children of those who stayed behind in the south."

So there are two types of black voters, but not a hundred factions?

When I did volunteer work for a civil rights organization in New York City circa 1982-1986, one of the first things I learned was that it was really hard to define a core set of characteristics, or cultural or economic or religious values, for any ethnic group. In fact, it's impossible.

Polling tends to assume otherwise. Polling assumes that the several hundred people who take a poll accurately represent a much larger number of voters, often several orders of magnitude. But ethnic background is only one factor which might influence one's vote, and is certainly complicated by age, income level, years as a citizen, first or second generation, etc.

How do you pull out ethnic background and ignore the co-dependency on so many other factors? Pollsters do it all the time. In fact, it's a good idea to keep all of these commandments on a slip of paper in your pocket during election season and refer to it early and often.

We'll go into a more specific example later. But here's what happens commandment by commandment with polling:

C-1: Polling is usually transparent only about statistical error. All others sources of error tend to be ignored, or obfuscated.

C-2: Pollsters have to make huge assumptions, but rarely illuminate them.

C-3: Polling involves many weak links which never seem to go away. For example, pollsters have cautioned for at least three election cycles that it is difficult to reach voters with cell phones. I invite you to think how many voters were missed this last time around because cell phone numbers are not public or how biased responses were because of too many land line respondents.

C-4: Past performance is almost always used to extrapolate how different groups will vote next time.

C-5: Pollsters love heat maps showing the country's red and blue voting tendencies. All they seem to do is confirm that large population centers vote blue and rural areas vote red. Question the picture!

C-6: Unfortunately, the business model of many "top" pollsters today is celebrity, not sober quantitative analysis.

C-7, C-12: Polls attempt to convert measures of sentiment into hard numbers even though sentiment is highly variable. Likewise, modeling the collective voting sentiment of a large human population is exceedingly difficult.

C-9: Models prove their worth when they predict something that occurs. So do pollsters. Their reputation grows when they "call it." But in a strange paradox, when models are correct, modelers are less inclined to tweak them. The better their reputation becomes as a result of past success, the less likely their continued success will be.

Finally, here's an observation about polling in presidential elections. The "spread" of statistical error always seemed to be +/-3 percent, which is an overall error of 6 percent. Knowing the last four election cycles were pretty close, and realizing, as the talking heads remind us over and over, the electorate is deeply divided, what does a poll with this much error really tell us in the first place?

In other words, the numbers are only confirming something we already know, not providing new insight. It's one thing to confirm an observation or a conclusion. It's another to waste so much time, energy, and money restating the obvious just because numbers seem to sound so much more impressive than thoughts.

And if you want to really see how numbers are used to inspire fear, stay tuned for the example in the next chapter.

17. THANK YOU FOR YOUR SERVICE

I read an article about how software is replacing high-level (and well paid) analysts at large financial engineering companies. The article references a study by two Oxford academics, claiming that "47 percent of current American jobs are at 'high risk' of being automated within the next twenty years."

First, would I even be paying attention if the study was conducted by academics at Southeastern Shore State College? Credential bias, commandment 9.

Three other elements of this article caught my eye: First, 47 percent is pretty definitive, i.e., it's not 'around 50 percent'. Second, twenty years is a long horizon of prediction; I always suspect anything over five years because it's virtually impossible for us to think beyond five years with a straight face. Forecasting farther out is like sitting on the beach, looking out to where the curvature of the earth cuts off your view and thinking, I know what's beyond that—without ever going out there to look.

I fetched the source paper referenced in the article. I have to confess, the abstract made me salivate. It appeared to be a perfect picture painted with numbers. After finishing it, I classified it further as abstract art.

Researchers developed a novel methodology to categorize occupations according to their "susceptibility to computerization." Second, they implement this methodology to estimate the probability of computerization for 702 detailed occupations. That's quite a number of occupations to study.

First, it is hard to be wrong with a "novel" methodology. Commandment 8 certainly comes into play: The (Co)mpany you keep will be pretty limited. The necessary broader validation won't be forthcoming until others accept and apply this methodology. I recognize this is what research is all about and these researchers I am quite sure don't intend for this paper to be the last word by any stretch on the subject. Yet think about what is meant by "susceptibility to computerization." How many parameters might affect the risk of a certain occupation becoming automated in the future and leaving workers unemployed?

One clue to the usefulness of this study (and the way the results are reported), is found near the end. Here is the verbatim quote: "According to our estimate, 47 percent of total US unemployment is in the high risk category, meaning that associated occupations are potentially automatable over some unspecified number of years, perhaps a decade or two."

I call your attention to the word "unspecified." And what do these researchers mean by "perhaps a decade or two?" Could we rephrase this as, the work supporting up to 50 percent of American workers is at risk of being automated in the future. "An unspecified number of years" is just a hedge using bigger words.

Also, I wonder how the journalist translated "an unspecified number of years, perhaps a decade or two" into "within the next 20 years?" This is no slight alteration or interpretation of the original source material.

The paper has a long section describing the math model used by the researchers. I won't bore you with it. I don't understand all the math myself. But it's easy to understand other aspects of the modeling from the text. Here are a few I pulled out:

The researchers state that the model algorithm successfully verifies subjective judgments about the computerization of an occupation based on nine variables they "eye-ball" as important to the automation process.

The researchers state that they "mitigate some of the subjective biases held by researchers by using objective [O-Net] variables to correct potential hand-labeling errors. The researchers acknowledge that "the hand-labeled version [of a key variable in the model] is a noise-corrupted version of the unknown true label."

The O-Net variables were developed by others to categorize an occupation's susceptibility to being shipped out of the country.

Central to the model is the selection of three "bottlenecks to computerization" and nine variables used to describe the potential for an occupation to be automated. They are finger dexterity, manual dexterity, cramped work space/awkward positions, originality, fine arts, social perceptiveness, negotiation, persuasion, and assisting/caring for others.

Now let's assess the possible violations of our commandments.

C-1: Acknowledge the error—researchers make no attempt in this paper to suggest how well they know what they think they learned; likewise for the journalists doing the reporting. What, for example, is meant by "noise-corrupted version of the unknown true label?" It sounds to me like a number so laden with potential error as to be potentially meaningless.

C-2: Identify the assumptions—clearly, many assumptions go into this study. One central to its validity is: characteristics used to assess whether a job is susceptible to being shipped overseas are good for assessing whether a job is subject to greater automation. I'm not sure this passes the smell test. Just because a job could be done with less expensive labor outside the country means that it could also be subject to greater automation? Perhaps, but perhaps not.

C-3: Weak links in the chain—I'd say this study is a very sophisticated attempt to do what I tried to do with my college rankings, that is, assign numbers to subjective criteria, feed them into a complicated equation, and hope no one looks too closely at how the sausage was made.

C-8: The (co)mpany it keeps—the results of this study are purely probabilistic. The statistical error can be known but all other sources of error are described in vague terms. It's hard to label this as more than a statistical correlation with questionable practical use, especially since the time horizon is equally as vague.

C-9: Would this study have made it into a "news source of record" if it had been conducted by researchers at the University of Southern Paducah instead of Oxford?

C-12: The automation of work is affected by numerous human system variables and progress with computers, automation, and robotics technologies. To what degree do we believe that the researchers captured them in this study?

This paper might have been more useful if it singled out one occupation and tried to validate the model's results with an experiment. If that experiment did validate the model, then they could apply the model to other occupations.

One example: The model suggests that cash register clerks are highly susceptible to automation. Any idiot who shops in a store has observed this. You can choose a checkout counter with no clerk and move your goods across the bar scanner yourself at most chain stores today. The researchers could have studied this one occupation, determined a rate of "clerk elimination" over the past twenty years, and extrapolated that into the future. This probably would have given a better estimate over a defined timeline than a probabilistic model.

The objective of this study appears to be to show at an aggregate national level what the impact of computerization would be on future employment. You can imagine policy-makers during important Congressional committee hearings listening to researchers from a prestigious university wondering, whatever are we going to do about the 50 percent of US employment opportunities which could disappear in two decades?

Modeling and numerical analysis have consequences.

Consider this thought experiment: Who do you think those legislators would take more seriously—these credentialed researchers or someone reporting on their experiences shopping at twenty big box stores over a five year period?

Now, if you think this example is troubling, the one in the next chapter will go one better!

18. A FAIR FOR ALL AND NO FAIR TO ANYONE

In high school, I was obsessed with the comedy troupe, Firesign Theatre, and the chapter title comes from a skit in which the comedians mock their experience in a Disney-like fantasy resort. The line came to me after pondering an academic paper with a highly mathematical treatment of fairness in commercial transactions. (Don't ask me where I find these things.)

Fairness, in this context, is the application of the Equal Rights doctrines to all citizens of the USA, regardless of ethnic background or socio-economic status, when applying for admission to college, a mortgage, a bank loan, insurance, credit cards, and other important lifestyle needs.

The paper describes a machine-learning algorithm which protects an entity who wishes to tailor a service to a customer based on her socio-economic characteristics without violating the customers equal rights or otherwise show prejudice towards the customer. A good example might be a credit card, which could have different interest rate levels, payment schedules, and minimums for a very credit-worthy customer than for a less credit-worthy customer.

It doesn't take a genius to see how difficult it would be to "quantify" fairness, at least to the extent that the seller can't be sued by an affirmative action attorney. The authors circumvent this little problem by using similarity as a proxy for fair. In other words, if two customers determined to be "similar" are treated the same way, then fairness has been achieved. That's the assumption, anyway.

Recall the discussion on measuring a parameter directly, measuring it indirectly using a proxy that correlates reasonably well, or assigning a value to a parameter. Direct measurements, proxy measurements, and assigned values are three different things.

What seems peculiar in this analysis is that the crux of the methodology is a hypothetical metric. What's more, the authors admit that the availability or practicality of this metric is the greatest challenge faced in their approach. Consider this passage from the abstract:

"The main conceptual contribution of this paper is a framework for fair classification comprising (1) a *hypothetical* [emphasis mine] task-specific metric for determining the degree to which individuals are similar with respect to the classification task at hand; (2) an algorithm for maximizing utility subject to the fairness constraints, that similar individuals are treated similarly."

Closer examination of the paper, and some deeper

interpretation, suggests that this violates commandment 11, starting with the answer and working backwards. The "answer" appears to be a system that protects the seller in tailoring products applied for on-line against accusations of bias based on ethnic characteristics or gender. In other words, the author's framework could be used to defend the seller's actions in the face of a legal challenge.

The answer was not to "achieve fairness in transactions" across classified groups of customers, including protected minorities. Similarly, the paper exemplifies commandment 6, the most important model is the business model. In this case, the numerical model appears to have been developed to serve the business model of the seller, not necessarily to protect the interests of its customers.

The numerical model is a means of allowing the seller to do what the seller always wants to do, maximize business success and profit from its customer base. In this case, the seller wants to continue offering products that maximize revenue based on the customer's socio-economic characteristics—without running afoul of affirmative action or equal rights laws.

Finally, consider commandment 7. Fairness is vague, hence the authors resort to the proxy, similarity. To a credit card company, how similar is one person to another? In this case, the similarity metric referred to by the authors includes something they call "distance," which essentially is a way to quantify how different one customer is from another. The authors "assume" that this distance parameter would be imposed by either a regulatory body or a civil rights organization.

Then there is this passage: "The similarity metric expresses ground truth." But here's the key: "When ground truth is unavailable, the metric may reflect the best available approximation as agreed upon by society."

Well, we can't say that authors violate commandment 2. They have made their assumptions transparent.

In the discussion at the end of the paper, the authors state "one of the most challenging aspects of our work is justifying the availability of a distance metric," and later the authors discuss approaches to building such a metric. What they appear to be admitting is they can't justify the assumption they made about the distance or similarity metric—that it is valid, or that it even exists. I conclude that the author's quantitative methodology is built around a hypothetical metric which relies on something "agreed upon by society." This is a pretty weak link to build a chain around, violating commandment 3.

Okay, enough with the vague academic exercises hoping to be practical quantitative tools when they mature. Let's get back to elections!

19. 'POLL' VAULTING IN MICHIGAN

Political science types will be analyzing the Trump phenomenon for years. It seems everyone got it wrong, even Trump, based on reports from the campaign on election day.

Unlike the geniuses portrayed in *The Big Short* who "called" (and profited handsomely from) the root cause of the great recession of 2007-2008, you had to look awfully hard to find the "contrarians" who were forecasting the Trump victory in the 2016 Republican primary and were proven correct. Based on everything I've read, the talking heads found one. Just one. You can, however, find a few celebrity pollsters who managed to tweak their analysis a few days before election day so that their predictions were "less wrong" when everyone woke up Wednesday morning.

A simpler exercise for our purposes is to examine the one state primary that pollsters really messed up (it turned out they also messed it up in the general election). They failed to forecast Bernie Sanders' win over Clinton, and instead had Clinton ahead by wide margins up until the polls closed. Even one highly regarded website known for the accuracy of its "poll of polls" methodology, was shocked by how much Sanders beat Clinton. What happened?

Some of the usual excuses (at least that I see) surfaced, that young voters were under-represented, that pollsters relied too much on probable voters with land lines (missing young voters who almost exclusively would be reached by cell phone), and that independent voters were not well-represented.

Polling exemplifies the fundamental principle of modeling. The less variability between the data used to create the model and the actual data used to predict an outcome, the more accurate the model will be. The characteristics of the people polled have to accurately represent the people who ultimately vote.

However, polling involves a subset several orders of magnitude smaller than the actual number of voters. Polling also usually involves applying general proportions as if they apply everywhere. For example, on a national basis, 37 percent of the electorate identifies as Democrats and 23 percent as Republicans, according to one source. That means 40 percent do not identify with either party. They are independents, a segment larger than either party. This really challenges pollsters.

In the general election, independents hold the key. The probability of a registered Republican voting

Democratic for President is slim to none; the reverse is true as well (although this is not true of the down ballot candidates where votes depend more on familiarity, resistance to change, attention paid to voters, pork barrel spending, etc.).

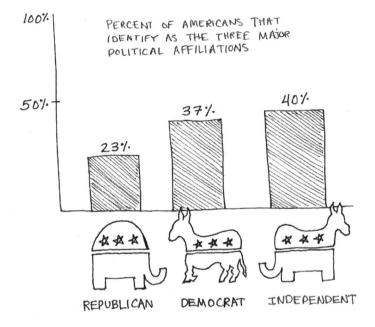

Figuring out what independents will do is no small task. They aren't called the swing vote for nothing. When 40 percent of the electorate can swing either way, polling may not even be relevant.

A pollster working the state primaries, for example, might just apply these percentages representing party affiliation for a state poll, rather than use actual measurements or data from that state (state level data may not even be available). The greater the swing vote, the riskier that assumption becomes. And who knows how old the data is on whether people identify as one party or another. That, after all, is known from polling small samples, and extrapolating to the larger population.

Speaking of affirmative action (from the previous chapter), many pollsters assume that minorities behave consistently, even identically. It's kind of ironic that a credit card company has to prove "similarity" to sell a customer a credit card on-line, but a pollster relies on similarity to make her forecast.

Michigan used to be a reliably "blue" state, generally voting for democratic candidates. As stated several times, it is easier to model something with little variability. These days, Michigan appears to be more "purple," suggesting it is difficult to rely on past performance for future results. This includes the likelihood of African Americans in Detroit metro voting for Clinton in the primary just because they did so in large numbers in 2008. Purple might also suggest that pollsters probe more deeply into those swinging independent voters.

In researching the Michigan "anomaly," I came across the American Association of Public Opinion Research Transparency Initiative. You might think this initiative focuses on the rigor or accuracy of polling methods. Nah! Instead, it simply compels those who subscribe to the initiative to disclose their methods.

An interesting potential flaw in conducting a meta-analysis of polls, or a survey of surveys, is that polls tend to converge on each other. If a Michigan poll showed Bernie ahead, and nine other polls showed him significantly behind, the outlying pollster might "adjust" towards the consensus view. The survey of surveys will only therefore pick up the consensus view.

In a postmortem of another top pollster's spectacular miss in the 2012 presidential election, company representatives wrote that they misidentified likely voters, under-counted Democratic leaning regions, over-counted whites, and when calling landlines, dialed only listed numbers, which skewed older and Republican.

It's hard to see what they got right.

But let's get back to Michigan. One pollster reported he had been polling the state correctly for three decades but got this one completely wrong. He also cited the landline-cellphone divide in the electorate. You get the feeling this cellphone problem is an Achilles heel of all polling.

None of this explains why all the pollsters got Michigan wrong but seemed to have done a pretty good job in most of the other states. In fairness, Sanders won by only a squeaker, 49.9 percent to 49.3 percent. But the polls had Clinton up by 20-30 points. It wasn't the size of Sanders win that was shocking. It was the size of the pollsters' error.

Commandment 4, past performance is no guarantee of future success, is probably the best takeaway here. Polling models which had worked in other states and in other elections simply didn't work this time. Not all anomalies can be accounted for.

In hindsight, as polling in the Michigan primary went, so went polling in the national election. But let's leave polling behind and get to my mother and her vitamins.

20. MOM KNOWS BEST—
OR DOES SHE?

I've taken vitamins regularly since early elementary school. I know it dates that far back because I remember how my mom found out all of her four kids were depositing the vitamins she gave us each morning into the trash on our way to the bus stop.

I've also been trying to determine almost all of my adult life whether these vitamins are helping me, hurting me, a colossal waste of money, or the price I've paid to alleviate the guilt I've harbored after deeply distressing my mom for that horrible behavior. At this point, I'd be plenty happy if someone just convinced me that taking vitamins all my life may not have a specific effect on a specific condition or ailment or future disease, but generally has been positive for my overall health. Even that "standard of benefit" can't be met.

By the way, I'm the poster child for those who don't need vitamins. I'm a very healthy guy. I'm also reasonably affluent. My vitals are well in line with healthy people. I exercise regularly, and I'm maniacal about consistency, though not obsessed with pushing myself beyond my limits (and hindering my health from injury). I "exercise for life," I tell people, not to compete, or prove I'm someone I'm not, like an athlete. Also, my family history lacks those diseases listed on the forms you have to fill out at the doctor's office. I watch what I eat and I eat a varied, widely recognized proper diet (skewed probably, toward a Mediterranean diet), and limit my intake of junk and soda. About the only area I may be borderline is alcohol consumption. I definitely hover around the two drink a day (average) standard. This is the only stat which raises an eyebrow with my GP during my annual checkup.

Unlike my sister, who swears the opposite about vitamins, not once have I been able to directly link taking specific vitamins with a change in a specific condition. Though I have taken Vitamin C more regularly than any other, I can't say that Vitamin C has truncated a cold/flu or prevented one. Not taking this vitamin hasn't ever prolonged a cold, such as if I were traveling and had no vitamins with me.

I suppose I could do what my father does—monitor and record my vitals every day, and describe anything relevant I am feeling or observing. But I don't. What's more, I have never been able to make the numbers add up one way or the other. Claims about vitamins I take include things such as: 1) more than a dozen studies show Vitamin C does nothing for the common cold; 2) Vitamin supplements increases mortality (my mother's been trying to kill me) ; 3) the case against multi-vitamins grows stronger; 4) a daily dose of multi-vitamins are an insurance policy if you're not getting proper nutrition for your diet; 5) there's insufficient evidence to determine if multi-vitamins prevent cardiovascular disease or cancer.

All of these sorts of claims are derived from nutritional studies, standardized and non-standardized tests and protocols, and deep nutritional and medical research. Some of the protocols may not have been customized for nutritional supplements, say some sources, so there may be "framework error" lurking about. However, the bottom line is that the short or long-term impacts of supplements are difficult to assess and the experiments almost impossible to design for credible extrapolation to larger population sets and other individuals.

The history of Vitamin C as a supplement can be traced back to Linus Pauling, an eminent scientist who won numerous world prizes (but who is also noted for having some "fringe" ideas). Because of his advocacy, Vitamin C became the "cure for what ails ya."

He certainly convinced my mother.

Vitamin popping is probably the best example of commandment 8, the (Co)mpany you keep. Am I healthy because I've taken vitamins all my life or am I genetically, biologically, and/or socio-economically lucky? (My parents are both physically healthy and active and are now in their late 80s/early 90s, although my mom might have a stroke after she reads this.)

It's very difficult to move across the spectrum from coincidence to correlation. But correlations can range from very insignificant to undeniable without ever moving into the realm of causation. For vitamin and nutrition studies, it is virtually impossible to weed out the effects of other parameters. Researchers try to do this by isolating one supplement to one condition, but this isn't a reflection of the reality of how each of our bodies functions in its own special way.

Linus Pauling originally reported on anecdotal experiments he conducted on himself. But he was a world-renowned scientist, so he got a pass because of commandment 9 and his credentials. His reputation preceded what many call his "dubious methods."

When it comes to nutrition, numerical analysis has completely and utterly failed me. I can't get near consensus, much less identify correlations, whether weak or strong, in the direction of benefit, harm, or neither. I suppose there is only (co)ld (co)mfort in my lifelong quest.

The previous examples have had a healthy dose of human system elements. So, let's move on to a physical system and see if the painting is any more insightful.

21. YOUR MACHINE WILL CRASH IN FORTY EIGHT HOURS

To show I am not just picking on those who design and apply models in the social sciences, and social networking arenas, I offer this example straight out of my consulting practice.

Earlier, I described the automobile oil life indicator. That indicator is all well and good, but let me ask you this: Have you ever blown a tire on the highway? Have you ever had to then limp along for miles with a flat tire? Wouldn't it give you peace of mind if your dashboard indicated *when* a tire is in danger of blowing? It'd be a damn sight more valuable than an oil life indicator based on mileage.

Modelers constantly seek such oil life indicators for much larger, and frankly, more dangerous and critical machines, such as those that power our electricity grid, transport heating fuel to our homes, process petroleum into gasoline, and are part of factories which make every product you can think of on a mass scale.

These machines require periodic maintenance and are occasionally subject to catastrophic failure. Such events cost millions and even tens and hundreds of millions of dollars. The final bill for the catastrophic failure of the Deepwater Horizon oil drilling rig in the Gulf of Mexico will be in the tens of billions of dollars.

Machines working in these high risk areas and facilities are outfitted with many instruments used to automate, monitor, and otherwise avoid catastrophic loss and forecast when maintenance is necessary. Yet big things can (and do) go wrong, sometimes in a matter of seconds.

Recently I met with a professor at a prestigious engineering institute who doubles as a consultant to industry. To prepare for the meeting, I reviewed a technical paper he had published more than ten years ago. The paper describes experimental work to develop an indicator of machine stability that essentially tells the operator how much margin is left before something adverse happens. For this type of huge, energetic machine, stability is critical.

The machine in my colleague's paper is commonly called a gas turbine, similar to the jet engines on commercial aircraft. For the purposes of this discussion, what you need to know is that this type of machine has sixteen combustors where the fuel is burned (think of the burners on your stove) and is connected to a generator which rotates at 3600 revolutions per minute. That's fast. The housing for this machine is as big as a modest home.

My colleague is researching a means of correlating combustor pressure to the combustor's stability, which is important for safety, efficiency, emissions, and avoiding catastrophic events. In his lab, he uses a single turbine combustor simulator to study the problem. His goal is to develop a model which will help owner/operators run their machines with less risk of unexpected failure. The model must be based on an accurate correlation between the pressure measurement and the phenomenon called "combustor stability." In this way, his clients could have the equivalent of that tire health indicator.

I'm going to reduce his very complex engineering and numerical assessment to two points. First, as he amply describes in his paper, to accomplish his goal, he needs a mathematical model of combustor oscillations. Several factors contribute to combustor oscillations, but let's simplify it to this:

$$CO = A + B + C + D + E$$

(where CO is combustor oscillation and
E is background noise)

With equations like this, one often finds that certain terms on the right side of the equal sign are negligible, at least for most situations. In model construction, this is common; the insignificant terms are ignored (in math terms, their values are assumed to be zero). Let's assume— that all-important, dangerous word in modeling)—that the equation is reduced to:

$$CO = A + B + E$$

It turns out that this equation can't be solved directly because there is a parameter which isn't known. Let's assume that parameter is B. The paper then says the equivalent of, "it is convenient to work with the autocorrelation of B." Now, I'm not exactly sure what he means by this, but I'm fairly certain he means a value that can serve as a proxy for B is inserted into the model. It is a way to estimate B, to approximate B.

The word proxy is a root in approximation.

These are the kinds of "fudge" factors usually demanded of models. In subsequent sections, the paper also highlights "key assumptions." Again, in my simplified explanation, E is also going to be ignored because its characteristics, i.e., its impacts on oscillations, are not well understood. Which isn't the same thing as negligible, but that's the way modeling works.

The second key point, and this is not a simplification of his work, is that his model has been constructed with one combustor. As mentioned, the gas turbine in the real world (where the phrase "objective reality" has meaning and consequences) could have up to sixteen combustors, all in close proximity to each other burning hundreds of pounds of fuel every minute. The paper acknowledges this and, further, acknowledges that there are interactions among the combustors, and that it isn't clear if subtle variations in the stability of one combustor may be distinguished from the variations of adjoining ones.

What we have here isn't dissimilar from several of the earlier examples. At this point in its development, my colleague's model is missing the context of a real-world machine. It's like something we discussed in an earlier chapter, taking that one parameter out of many which affect the condition under study and imposing a multiple regression analysis (MRA) on it out of context.

Notice also that the fundamental equation describing the phenomenon has been greatly simplified to construct the model. Also, the modeling will eventually have to be scaled up so that it accurately indicates something useful in a machine with sixteen combustors, not one.

Of course, he has to start somewhere; this is, after all, R&D. He is also fortunate, as implied by commandment 12, in that he is working with a physical system. As complex as a gas turbine is, it is going to be more predictable than one or more humans. You've got a far better chance of developing a model that indicates the likelihood of a gas turbine crashing in forty eight hours than you do one that indicates when the global economy will crash again.

And if my colleague's monitor eventually prevents one Deepwater Horizon event or similar disaster from occurring again, that will be, as they say, "priceless." The model will have done its job.

Well, I was hoping to refrain from going back to the gift that keeps on giving, but it's like addiction. It's just too tempting to beat to death the postmortem of this election season.

22. "DO YOU LIKE MY HAT?"

One of my favorite picture books as a little boy was *Go Dog Go!* by P.D. Eastman. In one frame, a lady canine, with a large elaborate hat (of the sort African-American ladies are known to wear to church on Sundays, British ladies are likely to be seen in at royal functions, and southern Belles are liable to sport at the Kentucky Derby), asks a male canine, "Do you like my hat?" The response is, "No, I do not like your hat!" They part company (but repeat the encounter several times throughout the story).

The image of those dogs came to mind when I became fixated on a candidate's favorability and unfavorability ratings. So, I looked up how a favorability rating is determined.

Apparently, the pollster calls up the participants in his/her carefully selected random sample and asks: "Would you describe your feelings for candidate A as favorable or unfavorable?" Or, "Do you have a favorable or unfavorable impression of how candidate A is doing her job?"

Imagine, the rating of the president of a country of

330-million people, leader of the free world, arbiter of the most powerful military on the planet, boiled down to this question.

It can't be that simple, can it? I dug a little deeper. Turns out, it can get more complicated. A pollster might ask his subjects to give the choice of mostly favorable, slightly favorable, slightly unfavorable, or mostly unfavorable. In the split second of a telephone poll, the respondent is asked to offer the sum total of an impression with these four choices.

I located a doctoral dissertation which studied whether negative advertising swayed voter opinion of McCain or Obama in the 2008 presidential election. The favorability rating used here was a five point scale ranging from very unfavorable to very favorable.

Recall how I opened this book with the college ranking system I fudged in high school and how it was little different from how "sophisticated" numerical modeling is conducted. Now I'm going to quote from the PhD thesis referenced above about their quantitative method:

> "To examine the contextual effects of political advertising environment on voters' candidate evaluations and vote choice certainty, we employed hierarchical linear modeling techniques using restricted maximum likelihood estimation with robust standard errors. We ran a series of random intercept models with micro- and macro-level predictors..." (p. 17)

Well, I won't bore you with the rest.

Whatever the fancy statistical and mathematical modeling, the results are based on very precise numbers (1, 2, 3, 4, 5) substituted for vague descriptors of favorability for which respondents have only a few seconds to decide.

"Do you like my hat?" Press 1 for yes, 2 for no.

DO YOU LIKE MY HAT ??

Violations of Commandments 3 and 5 are obvious. The vague characteristic of "favorability" is assigned values based on responses to a survey, the numbers are crunched, and a picture is painted of whether negative advertising swayed opinion in the 2012 US Presidential election. The measure of favorability appears to be weak indeed, but is propagated through some very complex math to arrive at results which can't be any better than the measure of favorability. That's because the weak link defines the strength of the chain, regardless of the gorgeous picture painted by a data artist.

CLOSING/POSTSCRIPT:
SEPARATION ANXIETY

Hopefully, the twelve commandments I've outlined and the violations I've illustrated using everyday examples will turn you into a numerical skeptic. Hopefully, you've seen how numbers can be strung together just like words, along a continuum from fiction to fact, and that you appreciate the long arduous road to an accepted quantitative or scientific "fact." Pictures of "reality" are painted using both words and numbers, and if you don't understand how the narrative is being spun, you're opening yourself up for manipulation by politicians, pollsters, businesses, scientists, etc.

By the time the information gets to us, it's been converted between words and numbers, perhaps several times, and massaged so much so that original information may not even be recognizable to the original researchers.

A researcher articulates a hypothesis or a theory, the hypothesis is converted into an experiment, data is taken during the experiment, a model results from the data, the model is validated using more data and more situations and its utility expanded. All of this is exchanged back and forth in the "expert" and professional community (or it should be) before it is reported to the non-expert, lay public, by gatekeepers called journalists, bloggers, Facebook friends, Tweeters, and others who may or may not have any earthly idea what they're talking about.

In other areas of modern society, models and algorithms are being used to automate our everyday lives, but typically on someone else's terms, not our own, even if that someone professes to have our "best interests" in mind.

I had the good fortune to publish a few academic papers on how financial engineering and an economy based on transactions have altered what constitutes a stock market (or any "market" for that matter), a company's balance sheet, accounting principles, financial reporting, economic activity, and the very foundations of capitalism.

My avocational interest in this subject was raised after the Enron and energy industry scandals of 2001-2003. It's an industry and a level of corruption I became intimately familiar with. By happenstance, I obtained a book (really a collection of papers presented at an academic conference) called *Accounting, the Social and the Political* (Elsevier Ltd, Oxford, 2005) and in this book was a chapter authored by Elton G. McGoun, Bucknell University, entitled "Hyperreal Finance." McGoun argues persuasively that finance in the real world had become hyperreal, meaning it had become an ends unto itself, rather than an activity integral to the real economy (the crash of 2007 certainly provided some evidence for this thesis).

I've observed this separation of value and activity in the electricity business (this is how McGoun and I started our conversation). The "exchange" value of investment vehicles and infrastructure assets had become separate and distinct from its "use" value. This has led to an economy in which wealth is not necessarily created, or not primarily created, through labor, reward, and savings, but through transacting. Value is no longer the intrinsic value of a power plant, the bricks and mortar in the ground. Instead, it becomes the inflated value of that facility for the next buyer, thereby maximizing the transactional value to the present owner, or seller, and all of the intermediaries to the transaction (bankers, lawyers, engineering assessors, etc.).

Infrastructure which used to be owned by one company for decades is now bought and sold five times in a decade. Stock prices no longer represent an intrinsic value of the company in question. To a large extent today, the stock price is the only value anyone recognizes for the company period. It has separated from its intrinsic, use, or natural value.

This is a phenomenon similar to the concept I described from *An Engine, Not a Camera* (see Appendix 1). The Black Scholes model for valuing an option wasn't developed to reflect (camera) the underlying value of an option, but to expand and drive (engine) a market for options in the first place. It was designed to help shape the reality of options trading, to create an atmosphere of comfort around the activity.

McGoun states that:

"Financial markets are the cause of changes in the real economy. Decisions affecting production and employment are made on the basis of the stock price, not on the basis of production and employment. It is not the 'real economy' that shapes 'reality,' but activity in the financial economy. The financial economy is thereby more 'real' than the real economy itself; it is a hyperreal economy." (p. 319)

In *Painting by Numbers*, I've tried to show that the lack of transparency around modeling and numerical analysis, whether in the financial industry, medical profession, politics, etc., has led to a similar separation of value and purpose. Most numerical analysis today is not intended to reflect for some stakeholder group or audience an objective reality or truth, or even work towards it. Instead, it is intended to shape our perception of reality. With social media and apps based on all kinds of algorithms, numerical analysis is quickly becoming our reality.

It isn't that financial engineering is bad; it should be a healthy component of the real economy. But the activity shouldn't be driving the real economy. Some reflection of actual firm value should be reflected in a stock price, not wanton speculation by professional financial engineers who extract a fee every time a financial instrument is bought or sold. By the same token, numerical analysis is an essential part of the betterment of society, but the more it drives people's perceptions, without people being conscious of it, the more dangerous it becomes.

In short, the less you know about numerical analysis, the higher risk you take of being victimized by it. Until there are better standards and practices in place for how numerical analysis is applied and disseminated, understanding this is a personal responsibility, not a collective one. It's up to you to know how well you think you know what you know.

Jason Makansi
Tucson, AZ, USA

APPENDIX 1

Other fine books on error, uncertainty, and bias; models and numerical analysis; and prediction/forecasting in our personal and professional lives

The Signal and the Noise, Nate Silver, Penguin Group, New York, New York, 2012.

This book should be considered a modern bible on the limitations of forecasting and prediction, but also on how prediction can be improved. I've recommended it to many friends and several have taken me up on it. If I ever teach a class on this subject, I will warm up the students with *Painting by Numbers* and then use *The Signal and the Noise* as the main text. The breadth of Silver's topics and discussion points are, well, breathtaking. He tackles numerical analysis in baseball, election polling, climate change, gambling, weather forecasting (different from climate change), epidemics, financial markets, chess and much more. If my work is known for one thing, I hope it will be that it achieved more with respect to brevity and simplification. *The Signal and the Noise* is an investment of time and brain cells but well worth the sacrifice of both.

Mindware: Tools for Smart Thinking, Richard E. Nisbett, Farrar, Strauss and Giroux, New York, New York, 2015.

I reference *Mindware* in the text, because of the author's unabashed warnings regarding the limitations of multiple regression analysis (MRA), perhaps the most prevalent numerical analysis conducted in research (especially the social sciences). Nisbett also observes that "our approach to hypothesis testing is flawed in that we're inclined to search only for evidence that would tend to confirm a theory while failing to search for evidence that would tend to disconfirm it." Nisbett's book is very readable. While his focus is on reasoning in general, experiments, and the philosophy of knowledge, his central question is very similar to mine: How well do we know what we know?

The Laws of Medicine: Field Notes from an Uncertain Science, Siddhartha Mukherjee, TED Books/Simon & Schuster, New York, 2015.

This slim volume, by the Pulitzer Prize winning author of *The Emperor of All Maladies*, reveals why 'the laws of medicine are really laws of uncertainty, imprecision, and incompleteness." They are, in fact, the 'laws of imperfection.' Probably the greatest piece of wisdom I got from this book is that even a perfect experiment is not necessarily generalizable. In other words, even if all of your statistics prove that your experiment ran perfectly, that doesn't mean your results can be extrapolated to larger or different populations or even repeated for an identical sample.

In my view, the medical profession is particularly rife with arrogance and inability to face the limits of certainty. Mukherjee courteously holds the collective profession up in front of a mirror, pointing out the flaws in what he concedes is a relatively young area of science.

Willful Ignorance: The Mismeasure of Uncertainty, Herbert Weisberg, John Wiley & Sons Inc, Hoboken, NJ, 2014.

Weisberg tackles the subject of uncertainty from the perspective of the general process of scientific discovery and uses engaging stories about scientists and "thinkers" throughout history to illustrate his points. Like Nisbett, he also thinks statistical analysis has approached "a crisis" (paraphrasing the back flap copy). One of his central tenets is that "this technology for interpreting evidence and generating conclusions has come to replace expert judgment to a large extent.

"Scientists no longer trust their own intuition and judgment enough to risk modest failure in the quest for great success." And this corollary: "Instead of serving as a adjunct to scientific reasoning, statistical methods today area widely perceived as a corrective to the many cognitive biases that often lead us astray." It isn't the role of science to provide answers; it's to refine the questions. It's a readable text but falls squarely between an academic textbook and one attempting to popularize science concepts.

Automate This, Christopher Steiner, Portfolio/Penguin, New York, New York, 2012.

The book's subtitle, "How Algorithms Came to Rule Our World," suggests that Steiner's focus is how human activities are being automated through bots governed by algorithms. "Algorithms," he writes,

> "operate much like decision trees, wherein the resolution to a complex problem, requiring consideration of a large set of variables, can be broken down to a long string of binary choices."

Binary choices are ones computers can make. But this statement also shows that an algorithm is just another form of numerical analysis. Of all the books I recommend, Steiner's scares me the most. Consider this:

> "Of the nearly one billion users in Facebook's system, the company stores up to a thousand pages of data, including the type of computer you use, your political views, your love relationships, your religion, last location, credit cards…"

(Remember, it was published in 2012).

Think about that with respect to the privacy vs. national security debate. At one time, the federal government forced AT&T to cooperate for national security in ways no one wants to remember. Now, imagine when the social media sites of our modern world have your information wrong, when they have drawn the wrong conclusions from your digital footprints! Steiner also describes a company which has developed a bot that "sucks in box scores from sporting events, identifies the most relevant aspects, and writes a story built around those aspects of the game. Is this the end of sports journalism as we know it?

Models.Behaving.Badly., Why Confusing Illusion with Reality Can Lead to Disaster, on Wall Street and in Life, Emanuel Derman, Free Press/Simon & Schuster, New York, New York, 2011.

Derman is a physicist turned Wall Street "quant" and was one of a plethora of authors weighing in on the financial crisis and great recession of 2007/2008. Derman brings into the discussion the idea of models and metaphors:

> "Models stand on someone else's feet. They are metaphors that compare the object of their attention to something else that it resembles. Resemblance is always partial, and so models necessarily simplify things and reduce the dimensions of the world."

But this later quote is priceless in its utility for understanding: "Once you understand that a model isn't the thing but rather an exaggeration of one aspect of the thing, you will be less surprised at its limitations."

This is similar to what Nisbett is trying to convey about MRA, which limits the researcher to one aspect of the thing, and thus loses the context of all the other influences on that one thing (e.g., a measured, independent variable). Although Derman focuses (mostly) on financial models, he explains very well the limitations of models for economics, global climate, and other broad situations compared to those used in physics.

An Engine, Not a Camera, Donald Mackenzie, The MIT Press, Cambridge, Mass., 2006.

If more people read and understood Mackenzie's account of his deep research into valuation models for financial derivatives and the inner workings of financial markets, the world of investment would probably be very different. Mackenzie shines a bright light on the purpose of most models—to create a version of reality and then capitalize on that reality. In this case, Mackenzie argues persuasively that the Black-Scholes model for options pricing, which did indeed by most accounts change the field of finance, was developed to drive a market (engine) rather than reflect a market (camera). His analysis lends evidence to a broader contention, that the "invisible hand" of the market is anything but, that markets are deliberately constructed for the entities which will participate in that market.

To my way of thinking, *An Engine, Not a Camera* is about uncertainty at its highest level, as it casts doubt on the entire notion of a "free market," "Markets are not forces of nature, they are human creations," he writes. To which I would add (as I suggest in the chapter on business models), models today are primarily used to create new markets and new realities, not expand our understanding of the human condition.

Useless Arithmetic, Orrin Pilkey and Linda Pilkey-Jarvis, Columbia University Press, New York, 2007.

This is an example of a book that focuses on a specific field of applications identified in the subtitle, "Why Environmental Scientists Can't Predict the Future." This quote sums up what you are going to learn from the Pilkeys: "The reliance on mathematical models has done tangible damage to our society in many ways. Bureaucrats who don't understand the limitations of modeled predictions often use them." Even if you consider yourself an environmentalist, Useless Arithmetic is very useful for understanding how math models are used and abused.

Merchants of Doubt, Naomi Oreskes and Erik M Conway, Bloomsbury Press, New York, 2010.

As I note, uncertainty is something used to create doubt. In particular, the authors take aim at scientists and researchers pressed into service (and well paid) to blow up what is left of scientific uncertainty on highly charged political and cultural issues to impede progress on the issues of the day. They go as far to accuse such experts as turning doubt into a "product." The issues they tackle include smoking and cancer, the ozone hole, global warming, acid rain, and other ecological issues. Unlike many of the other books listed, the authors in particular assess the public and political debates around these issues, not the scientific method. Health effects of smoking were turned into a great debate, funded by "big tobacco," after the scientific evidence was rapidly drawing the conclusion, assert the authors. Among the important tenets of wisdom imparted is that balance in reporting is not giving *equal* weight to both sides, but to give *accurate* weight to both sides. Some "sides" represent deliberate disinformation spread by well-organized and well-funded vested interests, or ideological denial of the facts.

Weapons of Math Destruction: How Big Data Increases Inequality and Threatens Democracy, Cathy O'Neil, Crown, New York, 2016.

You've probably inferred from the title that this book aims to be provocative and incendiary first. It certainly accomplishes that. O'Neil tackles data and modeling through the prism of social justice and power structures. But her metaphor is precious because it reveals how models evolve into WMD. One of her best examples is the *US News & World Report* college ranking system. Over several decades, it became the standard for college rank and therefore the object of intense manipulation so that colleges could improve on the rank. She observes (correctly in my mind) that all of the emphasis on the rating and its following among parents doesn't do a damn thing for the quality of education. When a school's objective becomes figuring out how to "game the ranking," it's no different than my attempt to game my rankings of colleges to favor the school I had already selected, as I illustrated in the opening chapter. O"Neil applies her analysis to getting insurance, landing a job, obtaining credit, on-line advertising and other aspects of unfairness in modern life.

An Introduction to Mathematical Modeling, Edward A Bender, Dover Publications, Mineola, NY, 1978.

Here, the term "introduction" refers to very mathematics-intensive theory and applications, optimization routines, and probabilities. The first chapter, "What is Modeling?" does a good job of laying the groundwork for those who wish to skip the math.

Measurements and Their Uncertainties, Ifan G. Hughes and Thomas P.A. Hase, Oxford University Press, Oxford, England, 2010.

This book, focused on error in physical sciences, also gets complicated in a hurry, but again, the first chapter is well structured and offers good foundational material. It starts with the overriding point that "there will always be error associated with that value due to experimental uncertainties." It goes on to classify uncertainties as random errors, systematic errors, and mistakes. While most discussions of uncertainty and error (mine included) focus on extrapolation, or extending a curve fit to data past the original measured data (or making inferences into the future using data from the past), this book reminds us that interpolation can be just as insidious. Interpolation refers to assuming the shape of the curve or line or graph between the measured data points. While this is a textbook, it is graphically rich rather than mathematically intensive (authors assume that computers will be doing most of the math).

Interpreting Data, Peter M Nardi, Pearson Education Inc, Boston, 2006.

This book keeps to the straight and narrow of how data analysis is applied in experiments. It notes in the introduction that "it is written in non-technical everyday language…" With passages like "Pearson r correlations are for interval or ratio levels of measurement… Many researchers, however, use these correlations for dichotomies and for ordinal measures, especially if there are equal-appearing intervals," I'm not convinced of the everyday language. Nevertheless, I found it useful as a refresher on how experiments are designed, data taken, results analyzed, and conclusions drawn.

A Demon of Our Own Design, Richard Bookstaber, John Wiley & Sons Inc, Hoboken, NJ 2007; and ***Lecturing Birds on Flying,*** Pablo Triana, John Wiley & Sons, Hoboken, NJ, 2009.

JASON MAKANSI

Both of these books are focused on financial engineering and were blessed in being well-timed with the collapse of financial markets and the world economy. They cover similar territory and both insinuate that financial markets are imperiled by the way modeling is applied. The subtitle for Demon is "Markets, Hedge Funds, and the Perils of Financial Innovation," and the subtitle for Lecturing Birds is "Can Mathematical Theories Destroy the Financial Markets?" However, everything I read tells me that things have only gotten worse, so unless you are seeking recent historical perspective, I'd supplement these two books with some more recent titles.

20% Chance of Rain, Richard B Jones, Amity Works, Connecticut, 1999

This book wants to be "Your Personal Guide to Risk," as its subtitle urges. Written by an industry colleague in my consulting work, who spent decades in the machinery insurance business, it's not really about modeling or uncertainties, but about risk and how we measure risk through probabilistic assessment. Jones stresses the uncertainty boundaries around any risk assessment and that "perception creates risk reality." He also offers this bit of timeless wisdom: "Statistics do not, and cannot, prove anything. The field of statistics is incapable of this. Statistics can provide information to help us make decisions, but the decisions are still ours to make." Today, statistics and numerical analysis in general are being used so decisions can be made for us (automation, digital algorithms, market construction, even on-line dating and hookup). We'd better all have a thorough understanding of their limitations.

APPENDIX 2

Specific articles and studies used in Section II. In no way do I want to cast aspersions on the journalists and authors of the articles and studies included below, but rather to use these examples to illustrate how we should all be better at understanding the implications of *Painting By Numbers*. If a chapter in Section II is not listed, a specific paper or article was not used or several were "genericized" to better articulate the point.

Chapter 14
Chattanooga Times Free Press, February 23, 2016

Chapter 15
"Male Sellers On EBay Have an Edge Over Women, Study Finds," *The New York Times*, February 19, 2016

Chapter 16
"Clinton, Sanders and Southern Voters," *The New York Times*, February 24, 2016

Chapter 17
Although my example was prompted by the article listed below (with source work cited next), the results and

implications of this study have been covered in numerous publications.

"The Robots are Coming for Wall Street," *The New York Times*, February 26, 2016

"The Future of Employment: How Susceptible Are Jobs to Computerization?*" Carl Benedikt Frey and Michael Osborne, Oxford Martin School, University of Oxford, UK, September 17, 2013

Chapter 18
"Fairness Through Awareness," Cynthia Dwork (Microsoft Research Silicon Valley, Mountain View, CA) and others, November 13, 2011

Chapter 19
http://www.aapor.org/Publications-Media/Press-Releases/AAPOR-Transparency-Initiative-Raises-the-Bar-for-P.aspx

Chapter 22
"Political Advertising Environment, Candidate Favorability, and Vote Choice Certainty in the 2008 Presidential Election: A Longitudinal Multilevel Analysis," Ming Wang (lead author) and others, Prepared for the 2010 Midwest Political Science Association Annual National Conference, Chicago, IL.

ACKNOWLEDGMENTS

Many thanks to the special friends and family who generously read and offered their feedback on early drafts, including Delal Makansi, Dr. Mark Hamilton, Dr. Elton (Skip) McGoun, Dr. Stephen Werner, Ronald Gombach, Mark Glaess, R Marshall, and Marv Stapleton.

And, to all the teachers, professors, authors, writers, analysts, consultants, executives, managers, colleagues, and friends who, after several decades, get you to a book like this one, thank you.

ABOUT THE AUTHOR

Jason Makansi has spent his entire career converting words to numbers and numbers to words. He earned his BS in Chemical Engineering from Columbia University in the City of New York, and has spent the last fifteen years as an independent consultant to the electricity industry for clients ranging from garage shop inventors to members of the Fortune 50 global energy corporations. A serial entrepreneur, he has raised venture capital for companies, launched and became Director of Research for a hedge fund focused on the electricity industry, led two Washington DC policy organizations, founded industry publications, started industry events, and authored dozens of industry level reports at the intersection of technology, policy, and finance. A sought-after speaker and thought leader, Makansi is the author of three professional books, the most recent the highly regarded *Lights Out: The Electricity Crisis, the Global Economy, and What It Means To You* (John Wiley & Sons, 2007). For several years, he pursued a higher degree in Sociology researching financial engineering and its impact on the economy and society. *Painting by Numbers* is the culmination of a career-long dream to get people more focused on error and uncertainty. He also writes and publishes fiction and has completed his first novel.